D1388313

Selected Poems

KATHLEEN RAINE

Selected Poems

GOLGONOOZA

PRESS

This edition first published 1988
Reprinted 1993, 2002

© Kathleen Raine 1988

Published by Golgonooza Press
3 Cambridge Drive, Ipswich IP2 9EP

British Library Cataloguing in Publication Data
Raine, Kathleen, 1908–
Selected poems
I. Title
821´.912
ISBN 0 903880 38 5

Typeset by Goodfellow & Egan, Cambridge
Printed at the Alden Press, Oxford

FOREWORD

---- ❋ ----

'Poetry is the house of the soul' I. A. Richards somewhere wrote, and that house we may build and furnish as we please; or partly so, for language is our human heritage, an ancestral domain others from time immemorial have created and tended. We must build our own poetic dwelling with words already laden with meanings, with the thoughts and values and dreams and hopes and fears of multitudes. Language is only briefly ours, whether we learn our words from the books of the wise or the speech of every day. So long as a civilisation exists we must work within the body of a language that has a life of its own; we inherit and transmit that life.

No one can suppose that the English language is any longer in its prime; words are worn thin with trivial use, emptied of meanings unknown to our materialist society. We are beset through press and media with a daily flood of words put to mean uses. Yet the soul still needs a roof over her head other than the breeze-blocks and acrylic paint of the world deemed real by media in the service of consumerism. No kitchen sink, however glossy, can tether the imagination. My mother, as she peeled the potatoes, inhabited her world of Border ballads, Shelley's skies, Milton's hells. The material commonplace, currently celebrated as the 'real' reality, has never been so for poetry, unless illumined by the soul's inner light. We pray indeed that this world may become 'as it is in heaven', that kingdom innate in all; but modern fashion would seem to reverse this rule of life, desolating the inner worlds and building the house of Psyche in the likeness of the mean, the meaningless and the vulgar. There is all too little in the secular city to remind the soul of her native country.

I was fortunate in having a country childhood, in growing

up to know birds, beasts and flowers, trees and streams, clouds and stars. 'Nature-poetry' is not what we write about nature, but rather the language of images in which nature daily speaks to us of the timeless, age-old mystery in which we participate. Nature communicates today what it told the earliest of humankind, and what it will tell future generations when our modern high-rise cities are no more. Meanings, moods, the whole scale of our inner experience, finds in nature the 'correspondences' through which we may know our boundless selves. Nature is the common, universal language, understood by all. I live now in London but here too the sun rises and sets, there is sky and clouds and rain, rainbows sometimes. Swans fly over the Thames and sparrows – blackbirds too – build on our drainpipes. I make no apology for writing in nature's age-old and unageing language, of whose images we build our paradises, Broceliande and Brindavan, the Forest of Arden, Xanadu, Shelley's skies, or even Wordsworth's Grasmere, which can be found on no map.

I suppose that I have written so that I may have a roof over my head in the invisible country. I would hope some poem of mine may sometimes shelter the solitude of others also, for the world of the imagination belongs to all. The 'I' of the poet is not 'me' (or so I would hope) but you also. If this is not so—when I do not speak from that deeper, that universal self all share—the poem has failed.

In writing poems I have but obeyed an inner impulse, as does the bird when it sings. Willa, Edwin Muir's widow, said, 'a poet must bear witness'; and W.B. Yeats's widow, George Yeats, reproached me, not for what I had written but for what I had *not* written: 'A poet has no right not to write' she said. I do not know at what behest, or for whom, I have written. The poet's writing hand transmits messages from the unknown to the unknown.

CONTENTS

From THE HOLLOW HILL, 1964

From THE OVAL PORTRAIT, 1977

From THE ORACLE IN THE HEART, 1978

Selected Poems

Night in Martindale

NOT in the rustle of water, the air's noise,
The roar of storm, the ominous birds, the cries—
The angel here speaks with a human voice.

Stone into man must grow, the human word
Carved by our whispers in the passing air
Is the authentic utterance of cloud,
The speech of flowing water, blowing wind,
Of silver moon and stunted juniper.

Words say waters flow,
Rocks weather, ferns wither, winds blow, times go—
I write the sun's Love, and the stars' No.

The Hyacinth

For James

TIME opens in a flower of bells
The mysteries of its hidden bed,
The altar of the ageless cells
Whose generations never have been dead.

So flower angels from the holy head,
So on the wand of darkness bright worlds hang.
Love laid the elements at the vital root,
Unhindered out of love these flowers spring.

The breath of life shapes darkness into leaves,
Each new born cell
Drinks from the star-filled well
The dark milk of the sky's peace.

The hyacinth springs on a dark star—
I see eternity give place to love.
It is the world unfolding into flower
The rose of life, the lily and the dove.

Nocturn

NIGHT comes, an angel stands
Measuring out the time of stars,
Still are the winds, and still the hours.

It would be peace to lie
Still in the still hours at the angel's feet,
Upon a star hung in a starry sky,
But hearts another measure beat.

Each body, wingless as it lies,
Sends out its butterfly of night
With delicate wings and jewelled eyes.

And some upon day's shores are cast,
And some in darkness lost
In waves beyond the world, where float
Somewhere the islands of the blest.

The Silver Stag

MY silver stag is fallen—on the grass
Under the birch-trees he lies, my king of the woods,
That I followed on the mountain, over the swift streams,
He is gone under the leaves, under the past.

On the horizon of the dawn he stood,
The target of my eager sight; that shone
Oh from the sun, or from my kindled heart—
Outlined in sky, shaped on the infinite.

What, so desiring, was my will with him,
What wished-for union of blood or thought
In single passion held us, hunter and victim?
Already gone, when into the branched woods I pursued him.

Mine he is now, my desired, my awaited, my beloved,
Quiet he lies, as I touch the contours of his proud head,
Mine, this horror, this carrion of the wood,
Already melting underground, into the air, out of the world.

Oh, the stillness, the peace about me
As the garden lives on, the flowers bloom,
The fine grass shimmers, the flies burn,
And the stream, the silver stream, runs by.

Lying for the last time down on the green ground
In farewell gesture of self-love, softly he curved
To rest the delicate foot that is in my hand,
Empty as a moth's discarded crysalis.

My bright yet blind desire, your end was this
Death, and my winged heart murderous
Is the world's broken heart, buried in his,
Between whose antlers starts the crucifix.

Angelus

I SEE the blue, the green, the golden and the red,
I have forgotten all the angel said.

The flower, the leaf, the meadow and the tree,
But of the words I have no memory.

I hear the swift, the martin, and the wren,
But what was told me, past all thought is gone.

The dove, the rainbow, echo, and the wind,
But of the meaning, all is out of mind.

Only I know he spoke the word that sings its way
In my blood streaming, over rocks to sea,

A word engraved in the bone, that burns within
To apotheosis the substance of a dream,

That living I shall never hear again,
Because I pass, I pass, while dreams remain.

In the Beck

For Anna

THERE is a fish that quivers in the pool,
Itself a shadow, but its shadow, clear.
Catch it again and again, it still is there.

Against the flowing stream, its life keeps pace
With death—the impulse and the flash of grace
Hiding in its stillness, moves, to be motionless.

No net will hold it—always it will return
When the ripples settle, and the sand—
It lives unmoved, equated with the stream,
As flowers are fit for air, man for his dream.

Vegetation

O NEVER harm the dreaming world,
The world of green, the world of leaves,
But let its million palms untold
The adoration of the trees.

It is a love in darkness wrought
Obedient to the unseen sun,
Longer than memory, a thought
Deeper than the graves of time.

The turning spindles of the cells
Weave a slow forest over space,
The dance of love, creation,
Out of time moves not a leaf,
And out of summer, not a shade.

On Leaving Ullswater

1

THE air is full of a farewell—
Deserted by the silver lake
Lies the wild world, overturned.
Cities rise where mountains fell,
The furnace where the phoenix burned.

2

THE lake is in my dream,
The tree is in my blood,
The past is in my bones,
The flowers of the wood
I love with long past loves.
I fear with many deaths
The presence of the night,
And in my memory read
The scripture of the leaves—
        Only myself how strange
        To the strange present come!

The Golden Leaf

THE floating of a leaf that fell
A wounded star upon the tide
Out of the world, free in farewell,

I saw—not able to withhold
The vanishing moment with my sight
From the lock of living heart,

And down the rapid nerves, the light
Plunged, where the thundering stream of blood
Engulphs each mote within the eye,

Upon the dark pool of my thought
Turned slowly, sinking into past,
Then poised on a reflected sky.

The Sphere

OH the happy ending, the happy ending
That the fugue promised, that love believed in,
That perfect star, that bright transfiguration,

Where has it vanished, now that the music is over,
The certainty of being, the heart in flower,
Ourselves, perfect at last, affirmed as what we are?

The world, the changing world stands still while lovers kiss,
And then moves on—what was our fugitive bliss,
The dancer's ecstasy, the vision, and the rose?

There is no end, no ending—steps of a dance, petals of flowers
Phrases of music, rays of the sun, the hours
Succeed each other, and the perfect sphere
Turns in our hearts the past and future, near and far,
Our single soul, atom, and universe.

The Moment

TO write down all I contain at this moment
  I would pour the desert through an hour-glass,
The sea through a water-clock,
Grain by grain and drop by drop
Let in the trackless, measureless, mutable seas and sands.

For earth's days and nights are breaking over me,
The tides and sands are running through me,
And I have only two hands and a heart to hold the desert
    and the sea.

What can I contain of it? It escapes and eludes me,
The tides wash me away,
The desert shifts under my feet.

Winter Solstice

EVERYWHERE
  The first bird of the year
Has sung a valentine
Tuned to the last winter star.

In cold shrill voice
The first loves of spring,
Leafless as the blooming
Of jasmine.

The stars' intervals
Lead in the first winds,
Open the first buds,
Hold the first pauses

That wait for hope,
Expectant of music,
Foreknowing leaves unfold,
Faithful to heart's beat.

The green winter stars
Of thistle and scabious
Open in slow cadence
Of the tall sweet flower,

The first light of dawn
On the heart's desolate stone
Will reveal a mountain
In a blue sky shining,

Each star is answering
Another, and the sun,
That bridegroom, kind once again,
Northward to me returning.

Word Made Flesh

WORD whose breath is the world-circling atmosphere,
Word that utters the world that turns the wind,
Word that articulates the bird that speeds upon the air,

Word that blazes out the trumpet of the sun,
Whose silence is the violin-music of the stars,
Whose melody is the dawn, and harmony the night,

Word traced in water of lakes, and light on water,
Light on still water, moving water, waterfall
And water colours of cloud, of dew, of spectral rain,

Word inscribed on stone, mountain range upon range of stone,
Word that is fire of the sun and fire within
Order of atoms, crystalline symmetry,

Grammar of five-fold rose and six-fold lily,
Spiral of leaves on a bough, helix of shells,
Rotation of twining plants on axes of darkness and light,

Instinctive wisdom of fish and lion and ram,
Rhythm of generation in flagellate and fern,
Flash of fin, beat of wing, heartbeat, beat of the dance,

Hieroglyph in whose exact precision is defined
Feather and insect-wing, refraction of multiple eyes,
Eyes of the creatures, oh myriadfold vision of the world,

Statement of mystery, how shall we name
A spirit clothed in world, a world made man?

Self

WHO am I, who
Speaks from the dust,
Who looks from the clay?

Who hears
For the mute stone,
For fragile water feels
With finger and bone?

Who for the forest breathes the evening,
Sees for the rose,
Who knows
What the bird sings?

Who am I, who for the sun fears
The demon dark,
In order holds
Atom and chaos?

Who out of nothingness has gazed
On the beloved face?

Quenching the Red

LOVE kindle,
  Death slay
Fires that consume
The earth away
Smoulder to black
The red clay.

Sun bleeds red
In the pit of the night,
The heart goes out,
And a black hand
Puts out the light.

The dragon-hole
Haunt of darkness
Swallows the world
And the hag's crutch
Buries the roses.

Death kindle
Love slay
The red man
In the black shadow
Behind the roses
Turns to clay.

The Journey

For Winifred Nicholson

AS I went over fossil hill
  I gathered up small jointed stones,

And I remembered the archaic sea
Where once these pebbles were my bones.

As I walked on the Roman wall
The wind blew southward from the pole.
Oh I have been that violence hurled
Against the ramparts of the world.

At nightfall in an empty kirk,
I felt the fear of all my deaths:
Shapes I had seen with animal eyes
Crowded the dark with mysteries.

I stood beside a tumbling beck
Where thistles grew upon a mound
That many a day had been my home,
Where now my heart rots in the ground.

I was the trout that haunts the pool,
The shadowy presence of the stream.
Of many many lives I leave
The scattered bone and broken wing.

I was the dying animal
Whose cold eye closes on a jagged thorn,
Whose carcass soon is choked with moss,
Whose skull is hidden by the fern.

My footprints sink in shifting sand
And barley-fields have drunk my blood,
My wisdom traced the spiral of a shell,
My labour raised a cairn upon a fell.

Far I have come and far must go,
In many a grave my sorrow lies,
But always from dead fingers grow
Flowers that I bless with living eyes.

The Traveller

A HUNDRED years I slept beneath a thorn
Until the tree was root and branches of my thought,
Until white petals blossomed in my crown.

A thousand years I floated in a lake
Until my brimful eye could hold
The scattered moonlight and the burning cloud.

Mine is the gaze that knows
Eyebright, asphodel, the briar rose.
I have seen the rainbow open, the sun close.

A wind that blows about the land
I have raised temples of snow, castles of sand
And left them empty as a dead hand.

A winged ephemerid I am born
With myriad eyes and glittering wings
That flames must wither or waters drown.

I must live, I must die,
I am the memory of all desire,
I am the world's ashes, and the kindling fire.

The World

IT burns in the void,
Nothing upholds it.
Still it travels.

Travelling the void
Upheld by burning
Nothing is still.

Burning it travels.
The void upholds it.
Still it is nothing.

Nothing it travels
A burning void
Upheld by stillness.

Peace of Mind

IF the pool were still
The reflected world
Of tottering houses,
The falling cities,
The quaking mountains
Would cohere on the surface

And stars invisible
To the troubled mind
Be seen in water
Drawn from the soul's
Bottomless well.

Spell Against Sorrow

WHO will take away
   Carry away sorrow,
Bear away grief?

Stream wash away
Float away sorrow,
Flow away, bear away
Wear away sorrow,
Carry away grief.

Mists hide away
Shroud my sorrow,
Cover the mountains,
Overcloud remembrance,
Hide away grief.

Earth take away
Make away sorrow,
Bury the lark's bones
Under the turf.
Bury my grief.

Black crow tear away
Rend away sorrow,
Talon and beak
Pluck out the heart
And the nerves of pain,
Tear away grief.

Sun take away
Melt away sorrow,
Dew lies grey,
Rain hangs on the grass,
Sun dry tears.

Sleep take away
Make away sorrow,
Take away the time,
Fade away place,
Carry me away
From the world of my sorrow.

Song sigh away
Breathe away sorrow,
Words tell away,
Spell away sorrow,
Charm away grief.

Spell to Bring Lost Creatures Home

HOME, home,
Wild birds home!
Lark to the grass,
Wren to the hedge,
Rooks to the tree-tops,
Swallow to the eaves,
Eagle to its crag
And raven to its stone,
All birds home!

Home, home,
Strayed ones home,
Rabbit to burrow
Fox to earth,
Mouse to the wainscot,
Rat to the barn,
Cattle to the byre,
Dog to the hearth,
All beasts home!

Home, home,
Wanderers home,
Cormorant to rock
Gulls from the storm
Boat to the harbour
Safe sail home!

Children home,
At evening home,
Boys and girls
From the roads come home,
Out of the rain
Sons come home,
From the gathering dusk,
Young ones home!

Home, home,
All souls home,
Dead to the graveyard,
Living to the lamplight,
Old to the fireside,
Girls from the twilight,
Babe to the breast
And heart to its haven,
Lost ones home!

The Unloved

I AM pure loneliness
 I am empty air
I am drifting cloud.

I have no form
I am boundless
I have no rest.

I have no house
I pass through places
I am indifferent wind.

I am the white bird
Flying away from land.
I am the horizon.

I am a wave
That will never reach the shore,

I am an empty shell
Cast up on the sand.

I am the moonlight
On the cottage with no roof.

I am the forgotten dead
In the broken vault on the hill.

I am the old man
Carrying his water in a pail.

I am light
Travelling in empty space.

I am a diminishing star
Speeding away
Out of the universe.

Amo Ergo Sum

BECAUSE I love
  The sun pours out its rays of living gold
  Pours out its gold and silver on the sea.

Because I love
      The earth upon her astral spindle winds
      Her ecstasy-producing dance.

Because I love
      Clouds travel on the winds through wide skies,
      Skies wide and beautiful, blue and deep.

Because I love
      Wind blows white sails,
      The wind blows over flowers, the sweet wind blows.

Because I love
      The ferns grow green, and green the grass, and green
      The transparent sunlit trees.

Because I love
      Larks rise up from the grass
      And all the leaves are full of singing birds.

Because I love
      The summer air quivers with a thousand wings,
      Myriads of jewelled eyes burn in the light.

Because I love
      The iridescent shells upon the sand
      Take forms as fine and intricate as thought.

Because I love
    There is an invisible way across the sky,
    Birds travel by that way, the sun and moon
    And all the stars travel that path by night.

Because I love
    There is a river flowing all night long.

Because I love
    All night the river flows into my sleep,
    Ten thousand living things are sleeping in my arms,
    And sleeping wake, and flowing are at rest.

Spell of Sleep

LET him be safe in sleep
    As leaves folded together
As young birds under wings
As the unopened flower.

Let him be hidden in sleep
As islands under rain,
As mountains within their clouds,
As hills in the mantle of dusk.

Let him be free in sleep
As the flowing tides of the sea,
As the travelling wind on the moor,
As the journeying stars in space.

Let him be upheld in sleep
As a cloud at rest on the air,
As sea-wrack under the waves
When the flowing tide covers all
And the shells' delicate lives
Open on the sea-floor.

Let him be healed in sleep
In the quiet waters of night
In the mirroring pool of dreams
Where memory returns in peace,
Where the troubled spirit grows wise
And the heart is comforted.

Two Invocations of Death

1

DEATH, I repent
Of these hands and feet
That for forty years
Have been my own
And I repent
Of flesh and bone,
Of heart and liver,
Of hair and skin—
Rid me, death,
Of face and form,
Of all that I am.

And I repent
Of the forms of thought,

The habit of mind
And heart crippled
By long-spent pain,
The memory-traces
Faded and worn
Of vanished places
And human faces
Not rightly seen
Or understood,
Rid me, death,
Of the words I have used.

Not this or that
But all is amiss
That I have done,
And I have seen
Sin and sorrow
Befoul the world—
Release me, death,
Forgive, remove
From place and time
The trace of all
That I have been.

2

FROM a place I came
That was never in time,
From the beat of a heart
That was never in pain.
The sun and the moon,
The wind and the world,
The song and the bird
Travelled my thought
Time out of mind.
Shall I know at last
My lost delight?

Tell me, death,
How long must I sorrow
My own sorrow?
While I remain
The world is ending,
Forests are falling,
Suns are fading,
While I am here
Now is ending
And in my arms
The living are dying.
Shall I come at last
To the lost beginning?

Words and words
Pour through my mind
Like sand in the shell
Of the ear's labyrinth,
The desert of brain's
Cities and solitudes,
Dreams, speculations
And vast forgetfulness.
Shall I learn at last
The lost meaning?

Oh my lost love
I have seen you fly
Away like a bird,
As a fish elude me,
A stone ignore me,
In a tree's maze
You have closed against me
The spaces of earth,
Prolonged to the stars'
Infinite distances,
With strange eyes
You have not known me,

Thorn you have wounded,
Fire you have burned
And talons torn me.
How long must I bear
Self and identity—
Shall I find at last
My lost being?

Message

LOOK, beloved child, into my eyes, see there
  Your self, mirrored in that living water
From whose deep pools all images of earth are born.
See, in the gaze that holds you dear
All that you were, are, and shall be for ever.
In recognition beyond time and seeming
Love knows the face that each soul turns towards heaven.

Three Poems on Illusion

1 THE MIRAGE

NO, I have seen the mirage tremble, seen how thin
  The veil stretched over apparent time and space
To make the habitable earth, the enclosed garden.

I saw on a bare hillside an ash-tree stand
And all its intricate branches suddenly
Failed, as I gazed, to be a tree,
And road and hillside failed to make a world.
Hill, tree, sky, distance, only seemed to be
And I saw nothing I could give a name,
Not any name known to the heart.

What failed? The retina received
The differing waves of light, or rays of darkness,
Eyes, hands, all senses brought me
Messages that lifelong I had believed.
Appearances that once composed reality.
Here turned to dust, to mist, to motes in the eye
Or like the reflection broken on a pool
The unrelated visual fragments foundered
On a commotion of those deeps
Where earth floats safe, when waves are still.

The living instrument
When fingers gently touch the strings,
Or when a quiet wind
Blows through the reed, makes music of birds,
Song, words, the human voice.
Too strong a blast,
A blow too heavy breaks and silences
The singer and the song;
A grief too violent
Wrecks the image of the world, on waves whose amplitude
Beats beyond the compass of the heart.

The waves subside, the image reassembles:
There was a tree once more, hills, and the world,
But I have seen the emptiness of air
Ready to swallow up the bird in its flight,
Or note of music, or winged word, the void
That traps the rabbit on cropped turf as in a snare,

Lies at the heart of the wren's warm living eggs,
In pollen dust of summer flowers, opens
Within the smallest seed of grass, the abyss
That now and always underlies the hills.

2 THE INSTRUMENT

DEATH, and it is broken,
The delicate apparatus of the mind,
Tactile, sensitive to light, responsive to sound,
The soul's instrument, tuned to earth's music,
Vibrant to all the waves that break on the shores of the world.

Perhaps soul only puts out a hand,
Antenna or pseudopodium, an extended touch
To receive the spectrum of colour, and the lower octave of pain,
Reaches down into the waves of nature
As a child dips an arm into the sea,
And death is the withdrawal of attention
That has discovered all it needs to know,
Or, if not all, enough for now,
If not enough, something to bear in mind.

And it may be that soul extends
Organs of sense
Tuned to waves here scarcely heard, or only
Heard distantly in dreams,
Worlds other otherwise than as stars,
Asteroids and suns are distant, in natural space.
The voices of angels reach us
Even now, and we touch one another
Sometimes, in love, with hands that are not hands,
With immaterial substance, with a body
Of interfusing thought, a living eye,
Spirit that passes unhindered through walls of stone
And walks upon those waves that we call ocean.

THEN, I had no doubt
That snowdrops, violets, all creatures, I myself
Were lovely, were loved, were love.
Look, they said,
And I had only to look deep into the heart,
Dark, deep into the violet, and there read,
Before I knew of any word for flower or love,
The flower, the love, the word.

They never wearied of telling their being; and I
Asked of the rose, only more rose, the violet
More violet; untouched by time
No flower withered or flame died,
But poised in its own eternity, until the looker moved
On to another flower, opening its entity.

I see them now across a void
Wider and deeper than time and space.
All that I have come to be
Lies between my heart and the rose,
The flame, the bird, the blade of grass.
The flowers are veiled;
And in a shadow-world, appearances
Pass across a great *toile vide*
Where the image flickers, vanishes,
Where nothing is, but only seems.
But still the mind, curious to pursue
Long followed them, as they withdrew
Deep within their inner distances,
Pulled the petals from flowers, the wings from flies,
Hunted the heart with a dissecting-knife
And scattered under a lens the dust of life;
But the remoter, stranger
Scales iridescent, cells, spindles, chromosomes,
Still merely are:
With hail, snow-crystals, mountains, stars,

Fox in the dusk, lightning, gnats in the evening air
They share the natural mystery,
Proclaim I AM, and remain nameless.

Sometimes from far away
They sign to me;
A violet smiles from the dim verge of darkness,
A raindrop hangs beckoning on the eaves,
And once, in long wet grass,
A young bird looked at me.
Their being is lovely, is love;
And if my love could cross the desert self
That lies between all that I am and all that is,
They would forgive and bless.

Three Poems of Incarnation

1

AT the day's end I found
Nightfall wrapped about a stone.

I took the cold stone in my hand,
The shadowy surfaces of life unwound,
And within I found
A bird's fine bone.

I warmed the relic in my hand
Until a living heart
Beat, and the tides flowed
Above, below, within.

There came a boat riding the storm of blood
And in the boat a child,

In the boat a child
Riding the waves of song,
Riding the waves of pain.

CHILD in a little boat
Come to the land
Child of the seals
Calf of the whale
Spawn of the octopus
Fledgeling of cormorant
Gannet and herring-gull,
Come from the sea,
Child of the sun,
Son of the sky.

Safely pass
The mouths of the water,
The mouths of night,
The teeth of the rocks,
The mouths of the wind,
Safely float
On the dangerous waves
Of an ocean sounding
Deeper than red
Darker than violet,
Safely cross
The ground-swell of pain
Of the waves that break
On the shores of the world.

Life everlasting
Love has prepared
The paths of your coming.
Plankton and nekton
Free-swimming pelagic
Spawn of the waters
Has brought you to birth
In the life-giving pools,
Spring had led you
Over the meadows
In fox's fur
Has nestled and warmed you,
With the houseless hare
In the rushes has sheltered
Warm under feathers
Of brooding wings
Safe has hidden
In the grass secretly
Clothed in disguise
Of beetle and grasshopper
Small has laid you
Under a stone
In the nest of the ants
Myriadfold scattered
In pollen of pine forests
Set you afloat
Like dust on the air
And winged in multitudes
Hatched by the sun
From the mud of rivers.

Newborn you have lain
In the arms of mothers,
You have drawn life
From a myriad breasts,
The mating of animals
Has not appalled you,

The longing of lovers
You have not betrayed,
You have come unscathed
From the field of battle
From famine and plague
You have lived undefiled,
In the gutters of cities
We have seen you dancing
Barefoot in villages,
You have been to school
But kept your wisdom.

Child in the little boat,
Come to the land,
Child of the seals.

3

WHO stands at my door in the storm and rain
On the threshold of being?
One who waits till you call him in
From the empty night.

Are you a stranger, out in the storm,
Or has my enemy found me out
On the edge of being?

I am no stranger who stands at the door
Nor enemy come in the secret night,
I am your child, in darkness and fear
On the verge of being.

Go back, my child, to the rain and the storm,
For in this house there is sorrow and pain
In the lonely night.

I will not go back for sorrow or pain,
For my true love weeps within
And waits for my coming.

Go back, my babe, to the vacant night
For in this house dwell sin and hate
On the verge of being.

I will not go back for hate or sin,
I will not go back for sorrow or pain,
For my true love mourns within
On the threshold of night.

Seventh Day

PASSIVE I lie, looking up through leaves,
An eye only, one of the eyes of earth
That open at a myriad points at the living surface.
Eyes that earth opens see and delight
Because of the leaves, because of the unfolding of the leaved,
The folding, veining, imbrication, fluttering, resting,
The green and deepending mainifold of the leaves.

Eyes of the earth know only delight
Untroubled by anything that I am, and I am nothing:
All that nature is, receive and recognize,
Pleased with the sky, the falling water and the flowers,
With bird and fish and the striations of stone.
Every natural form, living and moving
Delights these eyes that are no longer mine
That open upon earth and sky pure vision.
Nature sees, sees itself, is both seer and seen.

This is the divine repose, that watches
The ever-changing light and shadow, rock and sky and ocean.

The Marriage of Psyche

1 THE HOUSE

IN my love's house
There are hills and pastures carpeted with flowers,
His roof is the blue sky, his lamp the evening star,
The doors of his house are the winds, and the rain his curtain.
In his house are many mountains, each alone,
And islands where the sea-birds home.

In my love's house
There is a waterfall that flows all night
Down from the mountain summit where the snow lies
White in the shimmering blue of everlasting summer,
Down from the high crag where the eagle flies.
At his threshold the tides of ocean rise,
And the porpoise follows the shoals into still bays
Where starfish gleam on brown weed under still water.

In sleep I was born here
And waking found rivers and waves my servants,
Sun and cloud and winds, bird-messengers,
And all the flocks of his hills and shoals of his seas.
I rest, in the heat of the day, in the light shadow of leaves
And voices of air and water speak to me.
All this he has given me, whose face I have never seen,
But into whose all-enfolding arms I sink in sleep.

2 THE RING

HE has married me with a ring, a ring of bright water
Whose ripples travel from the heart of the sea,
He has married me with a ring of light, the glitter
Broadcast on the swift river.
He has married me with the sun's circle
Too dazzling to see, traced in summer sky.

He has crowned me with the wreath of white cloud
That gathers on the snowy summit of the mountain,
Ringed me round with the world-circling wind,
Bound me to the whirlwind's centre.
He has married me with the orbit of the moon
And with the boundless circle of the stars,
With the orbits that measure years, months, days and nights,
Set the tides flowing,
Command the winds to travel or be at rest.

At the ring's centre,
Spirit or angel troubling the still pool,
Causality not in nature,
Finger's touch that summons at a point, a moment
Stars and planets, life and light
Or gathers cloud about an apex of cold,
Transcendent touch of love summons world to being.

Shells

REACHING down arm-deep into bright water
I gathered on white sand under waves
Shells, drifted up on beaches where I alone
Inhabit a finite world of years and days.
I reached my arm down a myriad years
To gather treasure from the yester-millennial sea-floor,
Held in my fingers forms shaped on the day of creation.

Building their beauty in the three dimensions
Over which the world recedes away from us,
And in the fourth, that takes away ourselves
From moment to moment and from year to year

From first to last they remain in their continuous present.
The helix revolves like a timeless thought,
Instantaneous from apex to rim
Like a dance whose figure is limpet or murex, cowrie or
    golden winkle.

They sleep on the ocean floor like humming-tops
Whose music is the mother-of-pearl octave of the rainbow,
Harmonious shells that whisper for ever in our ears,
'The world that you inhabit has not yet been created'.

Rock

THERE is stone in me that knows stone,
  Substance of rock that remembers the unending unending
Simplicity of rest
While scorching suns and ice ages
Pass over rock-face swiftly as days.
In the longest time of all come the rock's changes,
Slowest of all rhythms, the pulsations
That raise from the planet's core the mountain ranges
And weather them down to sand on the sea-floor.

Remains in me record of rock's duration.
My ephemeral substance was still in the veins of the earth
    from the beginning,
Patient for its release, not questioning
When, when will come the flowering, the flowing,
The pulsing, the awakening, the taking wing,
The long longed-for night of the bridegroom's coming.

[50]

There is stone in me that knows stone,
Whose sole state is stasis
While the slow cycle of the stars whirls a world of rock
Through light-years where in nightmare I fall crying
'Must I travel fathomless distance for ever and ever?'
All that is in me of the rock, replies
'For ever, if it must be: be, and be still; endure'.

Water

THERE is a stream that flowed before the first beginning
Of bounding form that circumscribes
Protophyte and protozoon.
The passive permeable sea obeys,
Reflects, rises and falls as forces of moon and wind
Draw this way or that in weight of waves;
But the mutable water holds no trace
Of crest or ripple or whirlpool; the wave breaks,
Scatters in a thousand instantaneous drops
That fall in sphere and ovoid, film-spun bubbles
Upheld in momentary equilibrium of strain and stress
In the ever-changing network woven between stars.

When, in the flux, the first bounding membrane
Forms, like the memory-trace of a preceding state,
When the linked organic chain
Holds against current and tide its microcosm,
Of man's first disobedience, what first cause
Impresses with inherent being
Entities, selves, globules, vase-shapes, vortices,
Amoeboid, ovoid, pulsing or ciliate,
That check the flow of waters like forms of thought,

Pause, poised in the unremembering current
By what will to be fathered in the primal matrix?
The delicate tissue of life retains, bears
The stigmata, the trace, the signature, endures
The tension of the formative moment, withstands
The passive downward deathward streaming,
Leaps the falls, a salmon ascending, a tree growing.

But still the stream that flows down to stillness
Seeks the end-all of all waters,
Welcomes all solving, dissolving, undoing,
Returns, loses itself, loses self and bounds,
Body, identity, memory, sinks to forgetfulness,
The state of unknowing, unbeing,
The flux that precedes all life, that we reassume, dying,
Ceasing to trouble the flowing of things with the fleeting
Dream and hope and despair of this transient perilous selving.

The Moment

NEVER, never again
This moment, never
These slow ripples
Across smooth water,
Never again these
Clouds white and grey
In sky sharp crystalline
Blue as the tern's cry
Shrill in light air
Salt from the ocean,
Sweet from flowers.

Here coincide
The long histories
Of forms recurrent
That meet at a point
And part in a moment,
The rapid waves
Of wind and water
And slower rhythm
Of rock weathering
And land sinking.

In teeming pools
The life cycle
Of brown weed
Is intersecting
The frequencies
Of diverse shells
Each with its variant
Arc or spiral
Spun from a point
In tone and semitone
Of formal octave.

Here come soaring
White gulls
Leisurely wheeling
In air over islands
Sea pinks and salt grass,
Gannet and eider
Curlew and cormorant
Each a differing
Pattern of ecstasy
Recurring at nodes
In an on-flowing current,
The perpetual species,
Repeated, renewed
By the will of joy

In eggs lodged safe
On perilous ledges.

The sun that rises
Upon one earth
Sets on another.
Swiftly the flowers
Are waxing and waning,
The tall yellow iris
Unfolds its corolla
As primroses wither,
Scrolls of fern
Unroll and midges
Dance for an hour
In the evening air,
The brown moth
From its pupa emerges
And the lark's bones
Fall apart in the grass.

The sun that rose
From the sea this morning
Will never return,
For the broadcast light
That brightens the leaves
And glances on water
Will travel tonight
On its long journey
Out of the universe,
Never this sun,
This world, and never
Again this watcher.

Message from Home

DO you remember, when you were first a child,
Nothing in the world seemed strange to you?
You perceived, for the first time, shapes already familiar,
And seeing, you knew that you had always known
The lichen on the rock, fern-leaves, the flowers of thyme,
As if the elements newly met in your body,
Caught up into the momentary vortex of your living
Still kept the knowledge of a former state,
In you retained recollection of cloud and ocean,
The branching tree, the dancing flame.

Now when nature's darkness seems strange to you,
And you walk, an alien, in the streets of cities,
Remember earth breathed you into her with the air, with the
        sun's rays,
Laid you in her waters asleep, to dream
With the brown trout among the milfoil roots,
From substance of star and ocean fashioned you,
At the same source conceived you
As sun and foliage, fish and stream.

Of all created things the source is one,
Simple, single as love; remember
The cell and seed of life, the sphere
That is, of child, white bird, and small blue dragon-fly
Green fern, and the gold four-petalled tormentilla
The ultimate memory.
Each latent cell puts out a future,
Unfolds its differing complexity
As a tree puts forth leaves, and spins a fate
Fern-traced, bird-feathered, or fish-scaled.
Moss spreads its green film on the moist peat,
The germ of dragon-fly pulses into animation and takes wing

As the water-lily from the mud ascends on its ropy stem
To open a sweet white calyx to the sky.
Man, with farther to travel from his simplicity,
From the archaic moss, fish, and lily parts,
And into exile travels his long way.

As you leave Eden behind you, remember your home,
For as you remember back into your own being
You will not be alone; the first to greet you
Will be those children playing by the burn,
The otters will swim up to you in the bay,
The wild deer on the moor will run beside you.
Recollect more deeply, and the birds will come,
Fish rise to meet you in their silver shoals,
And darker, stranger, more mysterious lives
Will throng about you at the source
Where the tree's deepest roots drink from the abyss.

Nothing in that abyss is alien to you.
Sleep at the tree's root, where the night is spun
Into the stuff of worlds, listen to the winds,
The tides, and the night's harmonies, and know
All that you knew before you began to forget,
Before you became estranged from you own being,
Before you had too long parted from those other
More simple children, who have stayed at home
In meadow and island and forest, in sea and river.
Earth sends a mother's love after her exiled son,
Entrusting her message to the light and the air,
The wind and waves that carry your ship, the rain that falls,
The birds that call to you, and all the shoals
That swim in the natal waters of her ocean.

Night Thought

MY soul and I last night
Looked down together.
I said, 'Here we are come
'To the worst. Look down
'That chasm where all has fallen,
'The rose-bush and the garden
'And the ancestral hills,
'Every remembered stone.
'Of that first house
'There is no trace, none.
'You'll never cross that burn
'Again, nor the white strand
'Where lifted from the deep
'Shells lie upon the sand
'Or among sea-pinks blown,
'Never hear again
'Those wild sea-voices call,
'Eider and gull rejoicing.
'Turn away, turn
'From the closed door of home,
'You live there no longer,
'Nor shall again.
'You have no place at all
'Anywhere on earth
'That is your own, and none
'Calls you back again.'

Soul said, 'Before you were

'I spanned the abyss:
'Feedom it is, unbounded,
'Unbounded laughter. Come!'

Eudaimon

BOUND and free,
I to you, you to me,
We parted at the gate
Of childhood's house, I bound,
You free to ebb and flow
In that life-giving sea
In whose dark womb
I drowned.

In a dark night
In flight unbounded
You bore me bound
To my prison-house,
Whose window invisible bars
From mine your world.

Your life my death
Weeps in the night
Your freedom bound
To me, though bound still free
To leave my tomb,

On wings invisible
To span the night and all the stars,
Pure liquid and serene,
I you, you me,
There one; on earth alone
I lie, you free.

Night Sky

THERE came such clear opening of the night sky,
The deep glass of wonders, the dark mind
In unclouded gaze of the abyss
Opened like the expression of a face.
I looked into that clarity where all things are
End and beginning, and saw
My destiny there: 'So', I said, 'no other
'Was possible ever. This
'Is I. The pattern stands so for ever.'

What am I? Bound and bounded,
A pattern among the stars, a point in motion
Tracing my way. I am my way: it is I
I travel among the wonders.
Held in that gaze and known
In the eye of the abyss,
'Let it be so', I said,
And my heart laughed with joy
To know the death I must die.

Rose

GATHER while you may
Vapour of water, dust of earth, rose
Of air and water and light that comes and goes:
Over and over again the rose is woven.

Who knows the beginning?
In the vein in the sun in the rain

In the rock in the light in the night there is none.
What moves light over water? An impulse
Of rose like the delight of girl's breasts
When the nipples bud and grow a woman
Where was a child, a woman to bear
A child unbegun (is there
Anywhere one? Are the people of dreams
Waiting—where?—to be born?) Does the green
Bud rose without end contain?
Within green sepals, green cells, you find none.
The crude
Moist, hard, green and cold
Petal on petal unfolding rose from nowhere.

But the perfect form is moving
Through time, the rose is a transit, a wave that weaves
Water, and petals fall like notes in order;
No more rose on ground unbecome
Unwoven unwound are dust are formless
And the rose is over but where
Labours for ever the weaver of roses?

Bheinn Naomh

To Mary and John-Donald Macleod

1   SUN

SUN
Flashed from blades of salix of chitin of stone
Quiver of light on heather on hill on wings
Trembling makes one dazzling noon
Mirrored in rings of light that pulse in the burn

Glowing in eyes, throbbing in dust
Of butterflies dark as peat-pool brown
Endured in nerve, in ganglion in vein,
Budding of wings, leafing of lives
Myriadfold poised fragile on dark world lit with sight
Streaming undimmed, we suffer your joy
Poured down, down on in dark pools under
Overshadow of alder in undoing water.

2 GOLDEN FLOWERS

I HAVE travelled so fast that I have come to the waterfall of
    Sgriol:
Curtain of mist, of netted leaves, inviolate leafy vale,
Fragrant veil of green-gold birch and song of the green-gold
    linnet
A shadow withdrawn I enter for ever the sun-filled gloaming of
    Sgriol.

Light you have travelled so far out of the boundless void
From beyond the Isle of Skye over the sound of Sleat
You have laid a path of wonder over the bright sea
And touched with your finger the golden summit of Sgriol.

Water you have gathered in mist high over ben Sgriol,
So fast your drifting curtain of rain has fallen
That the noise of the sun-brown burn is filling the glen of Sgriol.

Seed you have grown so fast from the mould of the dead
You have unfolded a hundred flowers with golden petals,
The hundred-petalled golden flowers are filled with light
And leaves are moist with the life-giving waters of the burn of
    Sgriol.

Oh sun and water and green-gold flowers, I was here and now
    in the glen of Sgriol.

Light how fast you have travelled on into the abyss
And into ocean the burn that played in the sunlit fern of Sgriol.
Seed of miraculous flowers lies cold in the bog,
Sun sets in the beautiful land of the dead beyond the Isle of Skye.

3   THE LOCH

HIGH, high and still
Pale water mirrors
Thin air and still the high
Summit at rest in white
Water-spaces empty as thought.
The reeds wait
For ripple to trouble
Unsleeping gaze.
Nothing below it knows
But gathers the waters
That overflow
From the brim of reflection
Not all falls,
Soul remains
High and lonely
While blood runs
Down by the easy
Ways of sorrow.

4   THE SUMMIT

FARTHER than I have been
All is changed: no water for moist souls,
Wind and stone is the world of the summit, stone and rain,
Stone wind and cold, only the oldest things remain,
And wind unceasing has blown,
Without beginning or ending the wind has blown.

Noise of wind on rock cries to the soul 'Away,
'Away, what wilt thou do?' The butterfly

Blown up against the summit meets the snow.
Those who rise there endure
Dragon of stone and dragon of air; by wind irresistible
Hurled, or still as stone, the long way
A dream while the wing of a bird
Brushes a grain of quartz from the unmoved hill.

5 MAN

MAN on the mountain listens to star and stone:
Memory of earth and heaven
Lies open on the hill; sun moon and blood tell all.
The lonely voice that cried in the beginning
Calls in the belling of deer
And over the frozen lock unearthly music of the swan.
Thoughts of the dead are never silent
By the green mounds where houses stood,
Love and sorrow to come makes the air tremble.
Close as heartbeat is the word of the mountain,
Unsleeping the sky whose sight embraces all.

Childhood Memory

SUNSHINE in morning field,
Sunshining king-cups,
My flowers, my sun—
'But you cannot look at the sun,
'No one can look into the sun.'
And I said, 'I can,
'I can, it is golden, it is mine',
And looked into a dancing ball of blood,
A pulsing darkness blind with blood.

Sunshine in morning field,
Sunshining king-cups,
My sun, my flowers—
'But you cannot gather those flowers,
'The calyx in your hand is speed, is power,
'Is multitude; in grain of golden dust
'Smaller than point of needle, there they dance,
'Unnumbered constellations as the stars
'They spin, they whirl, their infinitesimal space
'Empty as night where suns burn out in space.'

Dear and familiar face
That beamed on childhood,
Shining on morning field and flower smile
What emptiness veiled,
Chasms of inhuman darkness veiled.

Lachesis

SOUL lonely comes and goes; for each our theme
We lonely must explore, lonely must dream
A story we each to ourselves must tell,
A book that as we read is written.

Our life a play of passion, says Raleigh's madrigal,
'Only we die, we die'; but older wisdom taught
That the dead change their garments and return,
Passing from sleep to sleep, from dream to dream.

In that life we dream, says Calderon, each soul
Is monster in the labyrinth of its own being.

Macbeth had his desire, an idiot's tale;
Yet the three fabulous spinners he had seen
Making from evil cause evil to come.

Oedipus' crime was greater, the murdered king
Where the three stories met being his father; yet
Blind when he saw, he came, a beggar and blind,
Honouring their mystery, to the gods
Whose life we die, living their death.

Dark lives are shades that make the picture bright,
Plotinus parabled; some born to sweet delight
And some to endless night, yet all are safe
As through those sweet or deadly dreams we pass,
Lost travellers all, Blake said; and Plato taught

That we ourselves have chosen what will befall.
In the Book of the Dead, the people of dreams,
By will and by compulsion drawn to birth
Live as punishment what each to live desires:
We are ourselves the evil dreams we suffer.

In what mind everlasting all is known,
Or in mind everlasting all forgotten
God knows, or maybe does not know, the Veda says;
Yet a few have seen the curtain drawn, and tell
With Juliana that all is well.

But what of that little bloodstained hand
Not all the bitter waves can wash,
Or the betraying hand dipped in the dish,
Predestined from the beginning of the world
And yet not guiltless, not forgiven?

Needs must these things be; and you and I,
My love, must suffer patiently what we are,
Those parts of guilt and grief we play
Who must about our necks the millstone bear.

The Hollow Hill

(Dun Aengus at Brugh na Boyne)

For Willa Muir

1

OUTSIDE, sun, frost, wind, rain,
Lichen, grass-root, bird-claw, scoring thorn
Wear away the stone that seals the tomb,
Erode the labyrinth inscribed in the stone,
Emblem of world and its unwinding
And inwinding volutions of the brain.
On the door out of the world the dead have left this sign.

The moving now has drawn its thread
Tracing the ravelled record of the dead
Through all the wanderings of the living.
Reaching at last the sum of our becoming,
The line inwound into a point again,
The spaces of the world full circle turn
Into the nought where all began.

We cannot look from the world into their house,
Or they look from their house into our sky;
For the low door where we crawl from world to world
Into the earth-cave bends and turns away
To close the hidden state of the dead from the light of day.
The grave is empty, they are gone:
In the last place they were, their clay
Clings crumbling to the roots of trees,
Whose fibres thread their way from earth to earth again.

Crouched in birth-posture in the cave
The ancestors are laid with the unborn,
(For who knows whether to die be not to live)
One worn hand touching the worn stone,

Calling the earth to witness, the other palm
Open to receive whatever falls:
Archaic icon of man's condition.

Yet so the great slabs have leaned three thousand years
That a single beam, shaft, arrow, ray
This dark house of the dead can pierce.
From world to world there is a needle's eye:
Light spans the heavens to find the punctum out,
To touch with finger of life a dead man's heart.

2

It is time, heart, to recall,
To recollect, regather all:
The grain is grown,
Reap what was sown
And bring into the barn your corn.

Those fields of childhood, tall
Meadow-grass and flowers small,
The elm whose dusky leaves
Patterned the sky with dreams innumerable
And labyrinthine vein and vine
And wandering tendrils green,
Have grown a seed so small
A single thought contains them all.

The white birds on their tireless wings return,
Spent feather, flesh and bone let fall,
And the blue distances of sea and sky
Close within the closing eye
As everywhere comes nowhere home.

Draw in my heart
Those golden rays whose threads of light
The visible veil of world have woven

And through the needle's eye
Upon that river bright
Travels the laden sun
Back from its voyage through the night.

We depart and part,
We fail and fall
Till love calls home
All who our separate lonely ways have gone.

3

THE rock is written with the sign
In geometric diamond prison,
Prism, cube and rhomboid, mineral grain,
The frozen world of rigid form
Inexorable in line and plane
At every point where meet and part
The cross-ways of the enduring world.

In curving vault and delicate cone
Each formula of shell and bone
In willow-spray and branching vein
In teleost's feathered skeleton,
In nerve of bird and human brain
Along its moving axis drawn
Each star of life has gone its way
Tracing the cross-ways of the world.

Here on death's door the hand of man
Has scored our history in the stone,
The emblematic branching tree
That crucifies to line and plane,
Writhes into life in nerve and vein,
Bleeds and runs and cowers and flies,
Resolved into a thought again
From nowhere come to nowhere gone

Those times and distances that span
The enduring cross-ways of the world.

4

THE tree of night is spangled with a thousand stars;
Plenum of inner spaces numberless
Of lives secret as leaves on night-elm,
Living maze of wisdom smaragdine
Opens in cell, in membrane, in chain in vein
Infinite number moving in waves that weave
In virgin vagina world-long forest of form,
Cold wild immaculate
Sanctuary of labyrinthine dream.
Lives throng the pleroma
Opening eyes and ears to listen:
Soft, soft they murmur mystery together.

O shadow-tree pinnate in a thousand leaf-ways,
Blades veined fine as insect-scales,
Glittering dust on soul's blue wing,
Full of eyes innumerable and senses fine
As feather green and the green linnet's song,
Arrow-swift wand in flight,
Pollen-grain on the wind
And bitter berry red,
Before you were, you are gone.

Gather a leaf blacker than night and bind it
Over the eye of the sun and the eye of the moon,
Closer than lid of blood, or lid of lead.
There is a banishing ritual for the world,
The great tree and its maze will shrivel
Smaller than pollen-grain, smaller than seed
Of bitter berry red: thought has no size at all;
And some in sorrow's well have seen
In daylight far stars glimmer pale.

WHITENESS of moonlight builds a house that is not there
On the bare hill,
Wide open house of night,
A gleaming house for those who are nowhere.

All there is valueless we value here,
Our houses are blacked out,
Things are dense darkness,
Nothing the silver surface of the night.
On black grass the untrodden dew is white,
On white birch black leaves glitter,
Bright rings scale the swift salmon river.

The house of the dead is alight,
The stones heaped over the cairn milk-white
In the mind's eye.
They say the charnel-house is a fairy-rath
But none knows where the dead are gone;
Yet when we turn away from a new grave
There is a lightness and a brightness
From those who have passed through the door that is nowhere.
Their death is over and done,
Ours still to come,
Grievous and life-long.
Not to be what we are,
Is it to be less, or more?
Waking, or dream, or dreamless sleep, nirvana
Is to be not this, not this.

A dying seabird standing where the burn runs to the shore
Between rank leaves and rough stone,
Its nictitating membrane down
Over eyes that knew a wild cold sky,
Head indrawn
Into neck-plumage and wing pinnae furled,
Disturbed in its dying becomes for the last time a gull,

Opens eyes on the world,
Brandishes harsh bill
And then withdraws again to live its death
And unbecome the gull-mask it was.

The dying are the initiates of mystery.
I have heard tell on lonely western shores
Of a light that travels the way the dead go by.
Upon an old door in his byre a MacKinnon saw it play
Where afterwards a dead man lay.
A MacIsaac watched it come over the sea
The way a young girl was rowed home from an isle.
It is a different light from ours, they say,
More beautiful.

They tell too of a darkness
That overwhelms and stifles flesh and blood
As the death-coach goes by,
For the living cannot travel by that invisible way;
But when a soul departs, a white bird flies:
Gull, gannet, tern or swan? Not these,
Another kind of bird
Into the emptiness untrammelled soars.

6

ONE night in a dream
The poet who had died a year ago
Led me up the ancient stair
Of an ancestral tower of stone.
Towards us out of the dark blew such sweet air
It was the warm breath of the spirit, I knew,
Fragrant with wild thyme that grew
In childhood's fields; he led me on,
Touched a thin partition, and was gone.
Beyond the fallen barrier
Bright over sweet meadows rose the sun.

[71]

The Path

I HAVE walked on waves of stone
Not knowing that the ground I trod
Is mirage in a watery glass,
A shimmering play of travelling light
Whose dangerous seas we call a world.
The shadow of the pleasure-dome
Midway floats, but deeper drown
All images on that surface cast.
Houses and cities seem and pass
On the meniscus of the flood.

There is a path over all waters
Leading to my feet alone
I have seen radiant from the sun
Setting beyond Skye and the more distant isles,
And rising over the rainbow seas of Greece.
It is the way to the sun's gate,
And I must walk that path of fire
That trembles, is scattered, reassembles
On all the sunlit moonlit waters of the world.

Dream-flowers

I N last night's dream who put into my hand
Two sprigs of verbena, culled from what sweet tree?
Your mother, it was told me, though I could not see her:
But to what daughter and by what mother,
By what Demeter to what Persephone given?
Was the hand mine that took those flowers

Given from one world to another?

There is a speech by none in this life spoken,
Yet we the speakers, we the listeners seem;
In that discourse, all signifies:
But what mind means the meaning that then is known?

Flowers of the earth grow out of the mystery;
From the deep loam of what has been
The past rises up in their life-stream
On whose surface images form and re-form;
But dreams rise up from a deeper spring:
Not from the past nor from the future come, but from the origin
These semblances of knowledge veiled in being.

Eileann Chanaidh

To Margaret and John Lorne Campbell of Canna

1 THE ANCIENT SPEECH

A GAELIC bard they praise who in fourteen adjectives
Named the one indivisible soul of his glen;
For what are the bens and the glens but manifold qualities,
Immeasurable complexities of soul?
What are these isles but a song sung by island voices?
The herdsman sings ancestral memories
And the song makes the singer wise,
But only while he sings
Songs that were old when the old themselves were young,
Songs of these hills only, and of no isles but these.
For other hills and isles this language has no words.

The mountains are like manna, for one day given,

To each his own:
Strangers have crossed the sound, but not the sound of the
    dark oarsmen
Or the golden-haired sons of kings,
Strangers whose thought is not formed to the cadence of
    waves,
Rhythm of the sickle, oar and milking-pail,
Whose words make loved things strange and small,
Emptied of all that made them heart-felt or bright.

Our words keep no faith with the soul of the world.

2 HIGHLAND GRAVEYARD

TODAY a fine old face has gone under the soil;
For generations past women hereabouts have borne
Her same name and stamp of feature.
Her brief identity was not her own
But theirs who formed and sent her out
To wear the proud bones of her clan, and live its story,
Who now receive back into the ground
Worn features of ancestral mould.

A dry-stone wall bounds off the dislimned clay
Of many an old face forgotten and young face gone
From boundless nature, sea and sky.
A wind-withered escalonia like a song
Of ancient tenderness lives on
Some woman's living fingers set as shelter for the dead, to tell
In evergreen unwritten leaves,
In scent of leaves in western rain
That one remembered who is herself forgotten.

Many songs they knew who now are silent.
Into their memories the dead are gone
Who haunt the living in an ancient tongue
Sung by old voices to the young,

Telling of sea and isles, of boat and byre and glen;
And from their music the living are reborn
Into a remembered land,
To call ancestral memories home
And all that ancient grief and love our own.

3 THE ISLAND CROSS

MEMORIES few and deep-grained
Simple and certain mark this Celtic stone
Cross eroded by wind and rain.
All but effaced the riding men, the strange beast,
Yet clear in their signature the ancient soul
Where these were native as to their hunting-hill.

Against grain of granite
Hardness of crystalline rock-form mineral
Form spiritual is countergrained, against nature traced
Man's memories of Paradise and hope of Heaven.
More complex than Patrick's emblem green trifoliate
Patterning the tree soul's windings interlace
Intricate without end its labyrinth.

Their features wind-worn and rain-wasted the man and
          woman
Stand, their rude mere selves
Exposed to the summers and winters of a thousand years.
The god on the cross is man of the same rude race,
By the same hand made from the enduring stone;
And all the winds and waves have not effaced
The vision by Adam seen, those forms of wisdom
From memory of mankind ineffaceable.

4 NAMELESS ISLETS

WHO dreams these isles,
Image bright in eyes

Of sea-birds circling rocky shores
Where waves beat upon rock, or rock-face smiles
Winter and summer, storm and fair?
In eyes of eider clear under ever-moving ripples the dart and
    tremor of life;
Bent-grass and wind-dried heather is a curlew's thought,
Gull gazes into being white and shell-strewn sands.

Joy harsh and strange traced in the dawn
A faint and far mirage; to souls archaic and cold
Sun-warmed stones and fish-giving sea were mother stern,
Stone omphalos, birth-caves dark, lost beyond recall.
Home is an image written in the soul,
To each its own: the new-born home to a memory,

Bird-souls, sea-souls, and with them bring anew
The isles that formed the souls, and souls the isles
Are ever building, shell by painted shell
And stone by glittering stone.
The isles are at rest in vision secret and wild,
And high the cliffs in eagle heart exult,
And warm the brown sea-wrack to the seals,
And lichened rocks gray in the buzzard's eye.

5   STONE ON HIGH CRAG

    STILL stone
    In heart of hill
    Here alone
    Hoodie and buzzard
    By ways of air
    Circling come.
    From far shine
    On wind-worn pinnacle
    Star and moon
    And sun, sun,

Wings bright in sun
Turn and return.

Centre of wing-spanned
Wheeling ways
Older than menhir
Lichen-roughened
Granite-grained
Rock-red
Rain-pocketed
Wind-buffeted
Heat-holding
Bird-whitened
Beak-worn
Insect-labyrinthine
Turf-embedded
Night-during
Race-remembered
Stands the known.

6 SHADOW

BECAUSE I see these mountains they are brought low,
Because I drink these waters they are bitter,
Because I tread these black rocks they are barren,
Because I have found these islands they are lost;
Upon seal and seabird dreaming their innocent world
My shadow has fallen.

The Halt

For Dorothy Carrington

TRAVELLING in trains of time, succession and causality
From sleep to sleep, from dream to dream we pass,
Desire from day to day drawing us on
But never bringing to our abiding-place,
For with our exiled selves we everywhere remain.

A long and ruinous track with many tunnels—
Such was the symbol given, the aspect worn.
The trains still ran, but not to my destination:
In distance and in time I had reached a stand-still.
It seemed that time itself was being dismantled,
For as I watched, the iron tracks were gone.

I had not reached the place to which I travel
Nor any place; a halt on the long journey:
Yet to be out of those trains seemed freedom restored,
My own free-will, fragile as life of wren or glass-blade,
And where the iron way had been there was earth
And rock fresh fallen from a mountain-side,
And mountain air to breathe.

If all this may seem,
Summoned up by the magician of the dreaming mind,
Why so meagre, why such bare soil, sharp rock,
Why this place scarcely a place at all?
Could not the dream have brought the traveller home
To the high unchanging country beyond time,
Given back the spring, the tree, the singing bird?
But dreams tell truth: I am not there
But at that very place I seem to be.

The Elementals

SAY I was where in dream I seemed to be
(Since seeming is a mode of being)
And by analogy say a curtain, veil or door,
A mist, a shadow, an image or a world was gone,
And other semblances behind appeared
Perhaps a seeming behind the real those giant presences,
But seemed reality behind a seeming
For they were fraught with power, beauty and awe:
The images before those meanings pale.

What seemed, then, was the world behind the world,
But just behind, and through the thinnest surface,
Not uncreated light nor deepest darkness,
But those abiding essences the rocks and hills and mountains
Are to themselves, and not to human sense.
Persons they appeared, but not personified;
Rather rock hill and crag are aspects worn:
Shape-shifters they are, appear and disappear,
Protean assume their guises and transformations
Each in as many forms as eyes behold.

They received me neither as kindred nor as stranger,
Neither welcome nor unwelcome was I in their world;
But I, an exile from their state and station
Made from the place of meeting and parting where I stood,
     the sign
Signature and emblem of the human
Condition of conflict, anguish, love and pain and death and joy,
And they in harmony obeyed the cross
Inscribed in the foundation of their world and mine.
From height to depth, circumference to centre
The primal ray, axis of world's darkness
Through all the planes of being descends into the prison of
     the rocks
Where elements in tumultuous voices wordless utter their wild
     credo.

The Wilderness

I CAME too late to the hills: they were swept bare
Winters before I was born of song and story,
Of spell or speech with power of oracle or invocation,

The great ash long dead by a roofless house, its branches rotten,
The voice of the crows an inarticulate cry,
And from the wells and springs the holy water ebbed away.

A child I ran in the wind on a withered moor
Crying out after those great presences who were not there,
Long lost in the forgetfulness of the forgotten.

Only the archaic forms themselves could tell
In sacred speech of hoodie on gray stone, or hawk in air,
Of Eden where the lonely rowan bends over the dark pool.

Yet I have glimpsed the bright mountain behind the mountain,
Knowledge under the leaves, tasted the bitter berries red,
Drunk water cold and clear from an inexhaustible hidden
       fountain.

The Star

I THOUGHT because I had looked into your eyes
And on our level eyebeams the world at rest
In motion turned upon its steady pole
That I had passed beyond the places and the times of sorrow.
My soul said to me, 'You have come home to here and now:
'Before all worlds this beam of love began, and it runs on

'And we and worlds are woven of its rays'.
But after I am in absence as before,
And my true love proved false as any other.
We looked away, and never looked again
Along the gaze that runs from love to love for ever:
So far? I wondered, looking at a star
Tonight above my house.

Eight Italian Poems

To Hubert and Lelia Howard

NATURA NATURANS

VEIL upon veil
Petal and shell and scale
The dancer of the whirling dance lets fall.

Visible veils the invisible
Reveal, conceal
In bodies that most resemble
The fleeting mind of nature never still.

A young princess
Sealed in the perfect signature of what she was
With her grave lips of silent dust imparts a mystery
Hidden two thousand years under the Appian Way.

A frond in the coal,
An angel traced upon a crumbling wall,
Empty chrysalids of that bright ephemerid the soul.

AGAIN this morning trembles on the swift stream the
    image of the sun
Dimmed and pulsing shadow insubstantial of the bright one
That scatters innumerable as eyes these discs of light scaling the
    water.
From a dream foolish and sorrowful I return to this day's
    morning
And words are said as the thread slips away of a ravelled story:
'The new-born have forgotten that great burden of pain
'World has endured before you came.'
A marble Eros sleeps in peace unbroken by the fountain
Out of what toils of ever-suffering love conceived?
Only the gods can bear our memories:
We in their lineaments serene
That look down on us with untroubled gaze
Fathom our own mind and what it is
Cleansed from the blood we shed, the deaths we die.

How many tears have traced those still unfading presences
Who on dim walls depict spirit's immortal joy?
They look from beyond time on sorrow upon sorrow of ours
And of our broken many our whole truth one angel tells,
Ingathers to its golden abiding form the light we scatter,
And winged with unconsuming fire our shattered image
    reassembles.
My load of memory is almost full;
But here and now I see once more mirrored the semblance of
    the radiant source
Whose image the fleet waters break but cannot bear away.

STATUES

THEY more than we are what we are,
    Serenity and joy
We lost or never found,
The forms of heart's desire,

We gave them what we could not keep,
We made them what we cannot be.

Their kingdom is our dream, but who can say
If they or we
Are dream or dreamer, signet or clay;
If the most perfect be most true
These faces pure, these bodies poised in thought
Are substance of our form,
And we the confused shadows cast.

Growing towards their prime, they take our years away,
And from our deaths they rise
Immortal in the life we lose.
The gods consume us, but restore
More than we were:
We love, that they may be,
They are, that we may know.

OLD PAINTINGS ON ITALIAN WALLS

WHO could have thought that men and women could feel
With consciousness so delicate such tender secret joy?
With finger-tips of touch as fine as music
They greet one another on viols of painted gold
Attuned to harmonies of world with world.
They sense, with inward look and breath withheld,
The stir of invisible presences
Upon the threshold of the human heart alighting,
Angels winged with air, with transparent light,
Archangels with wings of fire and faces veiled.
Their eyes gleam with wisdom radiant from an invisible sun.

Others contemplate the mysteries of sorrow.
Some have carried the stigmata, themselves icons
Depicting a passion no man as man can know,
We being ignorant of what we do.

And painted wounded hands are by the same knowledge
    formed,
Beyond the ragged ache that flesh can bear
And we with blunted mind and senses dulled endure.
Giotto's compassionate eyes, rapt in sympathy of grief
See the soul's wounds that hate has given to love,
And those which love must bear
With the spirit that suffers always and everywhere.

Those painted shapes stilled in perpetual adoration
Behold in visible form invisible essences
That hold their gaze entranced through centuries; and we
In true miraculous icons may see still what they see
Though the sacred lineaments grow faint, the outlines crumble
And the golden heavens grow dim
Where the Pantocrator shows in vain wounds once held
    precious.
Paint and stone will not hold them to our world
When those who once cast their bright shadows on these walls
Have faded from our ken, we from their knowledge fallen.

TRIAD

TO those who speak to the many deaf ears attend.
    To those who speak to one,
  In poet's song and voice of bird,
  Many listen; but the voice that speaks to none
  By all is heard:
  Sound of the wind, music of the stars, prophetic word.

DAISIES OF FLORENCE

BAMBINI picking daisies in the new spring grass
    Of the Boboli gardens
Now and now and now in rosy-petalled fingers hold
The multitude of time.

To the limits of the small and fine florets innumerable of white
    and gold
They know their daisies real.

Botticelli with daisies from the timeless fields of recollection
    scatters
That bright Elysium or Paradise
Whose flowers none can gather,
Where spirits golden immortal walk for ever
With her who moves through spring after spring in primavera
    robed,
Ripening the transient under her veil.

THE ETERNAL CHILD

A LITTLE child
    Enters by a secret door, alone,
Was not, and is,
Carrying his torch aflame.

In pilgrim cloak and hood
Many and many come,
Or is it the one child
Again and again?

What journey do they go,
What quest accomplish, task fulfil?
Whence they cannot say,
Whither we cannot tell,
And yet the way they know.

So many innocents,
Reflections in a torrent thrown:
Can any on these treacherous waters cast
Unmarred, unbroken,
Image the perfect one?

All things seem possible to the new-born;
But each one story tells, one dream
Leaves on the threshold of unbounded night
Where all return
Spent torch and pilgrim shroud.

SCALA COELI

WE do not see them come,
  Their great wings furled, their boundless forms infolded
Smaller than poppy-seed or grain of corn ·'
To enter the dimensions of our world,
In time to unfold what in eternity they are,
Each a great sun, but dwindled to a star
By the distances they have travelled.

Higher than cupola their bright ingress;
Presences vaster than the vault of night,
Incorporeal mental spaces infinite
Diminished to a point and to a moment brought
Through the everywhere and nowhere invisible door
By the many ways they know
The thoughts of wisdom pass.
In seed that drifts in air, or on the water's flow
They come to us down ages long as dreams
Or instantaneous as delight.

As from seed, tree flower and fruit
Grow and fade like a dissolving cloud,
Or as the impress of the wind
Makes waves and ripples spread,
They move unseen across our times and spaces.
We try to hold them, trace on walls
Of cave, cave-temple or monastic cell their shadows cast:
Animal-forms, warriors, dancers, winged angels, words of power
On precious leaves inscribed in gold or lapis lazuli,
Or arabesques in likeness of the ever-flowing.

They show us gardens of Paradise, holy mountains
Where water of life springs from rock or lion's mouth;
Walk with us unseen, put into our hands emblems,
An ear of corn, pine-cone, lotus, looking-glass or chalice;
As dolphin, peacock, hare or moth or serpent show themselves,
Or human-formed, a veiled bride, a boy bearing a torch,
Shrouded or robed or crowned, four-faced,
Sounding lyre or sistrum, or crying in bird-voices;
Water and dust and light
Reflect their images as they slowly come and swiftly pass.

We do no see them go
From visible into invisible like gossamer in the sun.
Bodies by spirit raised
Fall as dust to dust when the wind drops,
Moth-wing and chrysalis.
Those who live us and outlive us do not stay,
But leave empty their semblances, icons, bodies
Of long-enduring gold, or the fleet golden flower

On which the Buddha smiled.
In vain we look for them where others found them,
For by the vanishing stair of time immortals are for ever
      departing;
But while we gaze after the receding vision
Others are already descending through gates of ivory and horn.

Ninfa, April 1964

Soliloquy Upon Love

YOUR gift to me was a gray stone cast upon a wild shore,
    traced over
With calligraphy of inscrutable life. A marine annelid
With stroke as free as by master-brush, one fluent word
Has written with its life in the record of the logos,
Yet lacked senses to see its delicate coils and meanders of white
    masonry.
Mind unknown that blind plasm signed
With weight and drift of sea, of wave-refracted light, and stress
    of spirit
Omnipresent in every part, universal being here imprinted.
The number-loving Greeks built their white temples
To Apollo of the measured and Aphrodite the veiled source:
Does the same harmony inform those marble shells,
The word that is and means always and everywhere the same?
Your message of life to life was written on the sea-floor before
    we were;
Serpentine, strange and clear
The deep knowledge we share, who are not the knowers but
    the known.
You gave and I received as beauty what the logos writes:
Intelligible, though not to us, the inscription on the stone.

Euboea, 1965

A *House of Music*

To Margaret Fay Shaw Campbell

SOUND of music in the house,
Stir of intangible shapes that pass
Tracing in the awakened air
Meanders of melodious flow,
Waves that ripple on their course,
Meet and mingle, melt and part.

Those graceful forms your fingers rouse
Move like figures in a glass,
Dancing shapes that come and go
Purified in that silver pool,
Elusive of enamoured sense,
Yet mix and mingle with our thought;
And through our still reflections glide
Boucher's or Watteau's vanished France,
Treading in a *fête champêtre*
A measure in an April wood,
Dancers who are not flesh and blood
But spirits of harpsichord and flute.
Still in their own world they move
To Couperin's or to Rameau's skill.

Shakespeare's King Richard in his prison
Could not check the disordered tune
Of the sour discordant world;
But heard with the true inward ear
A concord that could mend his state,

[89]

Sweeten the music of men's lives
And bring his kingdom under rule.
Pythagoras could charm and lull
An ignorant homicidal rage
Awake the powers of the soul
To modulated harmonies
Our noise and violence drown and dull,
But still in nature's octave play.

The earth of Eden, I have read,
In some old wise forgotten page,
Is sound; and trees of Paradise
The woven music of that chord
Sung by the morning choir of stars;
Complexities that ebb and flow
From original concord grow
Texture perceptible to sense.
Let but once that music cease
Or discord mar those subtle forms,
Eden is a wilderness
The starry spaces barren ground.

Harmonious voices in the wind
Mould to their sound the listening ear,
Spirals that twine and intertwine
Tremble in the sensitive air
Till passive earth their imprint takes
And listens with an ear of clay
To that one Word the spirit speaks.

Caliban in his sleep could hear
Those island voices in a dream,
As all who listen are attuned
To shapes invisible but near
Men who rock upon the tide
Whose lift and fall their impress bears,
Or women at the close of day

Attentive to the blackbird's note
And wild sweet voices on the shore.

Canna House, April 1969

Letter to Pierre Emmanuel

C'est que l'âme française, qui habite même les plus déracinés, est une des grandes modes de l'intelligence et de la sensibilité humaines, indis-solublement. (From Pierre Emmanuel's speech on his election to the Académie Française, 1969)

'FRANCE, one of the great modes of the human mind and
    heart,
'Indissolubly', you have declared; for the souls of nations,
        as of men,
Abide in that Yonder beyond time, on whose frontiers we
        stray,
Looking for door or gate or breach in the wall, to enter,
        perhaps to return
(Paris—so many portals into green retreats and spacious
        chambers,
Expressive modes of subtle feeling and fine thought
Where we may sometimes find, or seem to find, that place),
But the life, as of a man, so of a city
(Near the Invalides a garden-hose dripping perpetual spray
On grass and philadelphus, where children play with sand,
Artist and poet with images, in the quiet shade)
Corruptible, soluble in time's flow,
'Paris', I too said on a June day in nineteen sixty-nine,
'Never from the beginning of the world to the end of time
'Has been or will be so great a city dreamed by man'.

[91]

To be a barbarian is to have no past;
For the past is the present of the future, the human kingdom;
Some known to us, others unknown, you, I, that still
    continuing few
To those hearts the remembered and forgotten dead are
    presences,
Ripening in memory the seed of cities
To scatter for what meagre crop this poisoned stricken earth may
    bear,
Keep France, keep Christendom, keep Athens in mind.

Here at Royaumont a plaster Gothic angel on the stair,
Image of an image, with slender finger points a delicate
    half-forgotten heaven
To us who in a present far from that presence come and go
While the sun of yet one more summer
Opens centifoliate roses on the still standing wall
Of this reason-ruined house of God raised by the genius and
    the kings of France
Whose sanctuary the first shock of the Terror to come, laid
    low.

A Painting by Winifred Nicholson

SUNLIT green of a late summer hayfield
(The pikes all led and their faint circles faded)
Sheltered by abundant beech, goldening to autumn fire,
And beyond, soft English hills that close the view.
Some happy hand has gathered cistus, bergamot, scabious
From the untidy sheltered brick-walled border,
Taken a jug from the flower-room, and put them, just as they
    were,
(Giving them a little shake to free their plumage)
By the window, where a passing bee or butterfly may come.

'That is an old picture', my friend said;
And I, 'How like the real world you and I remember'.
—For those same peaceful fields of vanished summer
Were spread alike for ladies of the castle
And for the niece of the village schoolteacher.

Fields, it is true, in the aftermath are still green,
Beeches turn brown, country flowers in unheeded gardens grow.
It is something else, we said, that will not come again,

That leisure, that ease of heart unsevered from its roots;
The things we thought about, some sweetness in the air, nuance
Of educated English speech, libraries, country lanes;
Few cars; 'wireless' a cat's whisker and a piece of quartz
Boys fiddled with. But there was laughter,
Songs at the piano, the Golden Bough, the Spirit of Man;
Pressed flowers; how fondly we took civilisation for granted!

Bank's Head, October 1968

Childhood

I SEE all, am all, all.
I leap along the line of the horizon hill,
I am a cloud in the high sky,
I trace the veins of intricate fern,
In the dark ivy wall the wren's world
Soft to bird breast nest of round eggs is mine,
Mine in the rowan-tree the blackbird's thought
Inviolate in leaves ensphered.
I am bird-world, leaf-life, I am wasp-world hung
Under low berry-branch of hidden thorn,
Friable paper-world humming with hate,
Moss-thought, rain-thought, stone still thought on the hill.

Never, never, never will I go home to be a child.

By the River Eden

1

NEVER twice that river
Though the still turning water
In its dark pools
Mirrors suspended green
Of an unchanging scene.

Frail bubbles revolve,
Break in the rippling falls,
The same, I could believe,
Each with its moment gone,
I watched in former years,

Ever-reforming maze
Of evening midge's dance,
Swifts that chase and scream
Touching in their low flight
The picture on the stream.

Heart is deceived,
Or knows what mind ignores:
Not the mirroring flux
Nor mirrored scene remain
Nor the rocky bed
Of the river's course,

But shadows intangible
That fade and come again.
Through their enduring forms
The glassy river runs;
All flows save the image
Cast on that shimmering screen.

BESIDE the river Eden
Some child has made her secret garden
On an alder strand
Marked out with pebbles in the sand,
Patterned with meadow flowers,
As once I did, and was.

My mother who from time past
Recalls the red spots on the yellow mimulus
That nodded in the burn
To her alone
Was that same child,

And hers, bedridden,
Mused on an old cracked darkened picture of
     a salmon-river
Painted in Paradise so long ago
None living ever saw those tumbling waters flow.
By her imagination made miraculous
Water of life poured over its faded varnished
     stones.

All is one, I or another,
She was I, she was my mother,
The same child for ever
Building the same green bower by the same river.

<h2 style="text-align:center">3</h2>

THE lapwing's wavering flight
Warns me from her nest,
Her wild sanctuary;
Dark wings, white breast.
The Nine Nicks have weathered,
Lichened slabs tumbled,
In sand under roots of thyme

Bone and feather lie,
The ceaseless wind has blown;
But over my gray head
The plover's unageing cry.

Heirloom

SHE gave me childhood's flowers,
Heather and wild thyme,
Eyebright and tormentil,
Lichen's mealy cup
Dry on wind-scored stone,
The corbies on the rock,
The rowan by the burn.

Sea-marvels a child beheld
Out in the fisherman's boat,
Fringed pulsing violet
Medusa, sea-gooseberries,
Starfish on the sea-floor,
Cowries and rainbow-shells
From pools on a rocky shore,

Gave me her memories,
But kept her last treasure:
'When I was a lass', she said,
'Sitting among the heather,
'Suddenly I saw
'That all the moor was alive!
'I have told no one before'.

That was my mother's tale.
Seventy years had gone

Since she saw the living skein
Of which the world is woven,
And having seen, knew all;
Through long indifferent years
Treasuring the priceless pearl.

The Return

I HAVE come back to ancient shores where it is always now.
The beautiful troubled waters breaking over the skerry
On the wind in spindrift blown like lifting hair,
Clouds gathering over the summits of Rhum in the clear blue
Are as they were
When long ago I went my way in sorrow.
Time, measure of absence, is not here—
In the wide present of the sky
Fleet the broadcast light is already returning, while we,
Who tell the hours and days by the beat of a heart
Can only depart
After a vanishing radiance dragging mortal feet.
But joy outspeeds light's wheel, the moments in their flight
Stays, here where in patterned strands the weed holds fast to
      the shore,
Falls and lifts from ebb to flow
Of the unceasing tide that makes all things new,
And the curlew with immortal voices cry.

APRIL'S new apple buds on an old lichened tree;
Slender shadows quiver, celandines burn in the orchard
    grass—
This moment's image: how long does a moment stay?
I took, and look away, and look again, and see
The morning light has changed a little, the linnet flown;
    but who can say
When one moment's present became the next moment's past
To which this now was still the yet-to-be?
It seems, in this old walled garden, time does not pass,

Only mind wanders and returns; I watch attentively
And see not one green blade move out of its place.
The Easter daffodils, the shadows and the apple-trees
Phrases in music continuous from first to last.
To be is to be always here and now.
The green linnet flits from bough to bough.

Canna House, 27 April 1969

I FELT, under my old breasts, this April day,
Young breasts, like leaf and flower to come, under gray
    apple-buds
And heard a young girl within me say,
'Let me be free of this winter bark, this toil-worn body,
'I who am young,
'My form subtle as a dream'.
And I replied, 'You, who are I,
'Entered a sad house when you put on my clay.
'This shabby menial self, and life-long time,
'Bear with as you may
'Until your ripening joy
'Put off the dust and ashes that I am,
'Like winter scales cast from the living tree.'

[98]

There shall be no more Sea

THESE rolling flowing plunging breaking everlasting
  weaving waters
Moved by tumultuous invisible currents of the air
Seem liquid light, seem flaming sun-ocean pouring fire,
And the heavy streaming windbeaten waves
Consubstantial with glint and gold-dazzle flashed from glassy
    crests.
On turbulence of light we float.

Why then should I not walk on water? Through water-walls
Of intangible light, mirage through mirage pass?
This body solid and visible to sense
Insubstantial as the shouting host of the changeable wind
Or fluent forms that plunge under wave, embrace passing
    through embrace.
Melting merging parting for ever,
Or oreads slender as a line of shadow moving across
    mountain's roseate face.

On an Ancient Isle

SO like, they seem the same,
  The young shoots of the yellow iris sheathed leaf through
    leaf,
Lit green of glittering blades and shadows quivering on the
    sanded turf
Where limpet shells are strewn among the celandine
And driftwood from the surf.
So like they seem, almost I to my own memories had come
    home.

Never green leaf nor golden flower again;
Yet from the one immaculate root spring after spring
Upon this farthest Western shore the one Paradise,
Earth sea and sky patterned with the one dream,
Traced on the wild that legendary land
More ancient than song or story or carved stone
My mother and her mother's mother knew: the green ways,
Clear wells, stones of power, presences
In hoodie's shape, high distant summits, hosts in the wind.
Signs in a language more heartfelt than holy book, or rune,
Each hill and hollow, each moving wing or shadow, means.
'Memory pours through the womb and lives in the air,'
And childhood with new eyes sees the for ever known:
The words by heart, we live the story as we will.

As I came over the hill to an unvisited shore
I seemed, though old, at the untold beginning of a familiar tale.

The Dead

NOT because they are far, but because so near
   The dead seem strange to us;
Stripped of those unprized familiar forms they wore,
Defending from our power to wound
That poignant naked thing they were,
The holy souls
Speak, essence to essence, heart to heart.
Scarcely can we dare
To know in such intimacy
Those whom courtesy, or reticence, or fear
Hid, when, covered in skins of beasts,
Evading and evaded,

We turned the faces of our souls away.
Only the youngest child is as near as they,
Or those who share the marriage-bed
When pity and tenderness dwell there.

Falling Leaves

WHIRLED dust, world dust,
Tossed and torn from trees,
No more they labour for life, no more
Shelter of green glade, shade
Of apples under leaf, lifted in air
They soar, no longer leaves.

What, wind that bears me,
Am I about to be? Will water
Draw me down among its multitude?
Earth shall I return, shall I return to the tree?
Or by fire go further
From myself than now I can know or dare?

LONG ago I thought you young, bright daimon,
Whisperer in my ear
Of springs of water, leaves and song of birds,
By all time younger
Than I, who from the day of my conception
Began to age into experience and pain;
But now life in its cycle swings out of time again

I see how old you were,
Older by eternity than I, who, my hair gray,
Eyes dim with reading books,
Can never fathom those grave deep memories
Whose messenger you are,
Day-spring to the young, and to the old, ancient of days.

Paris, 30 April 1968

Dreams

ONCE upon earth they stood,
Tree and miraculous bird,
Water from holy well,
Lamp whose undying flame
Burns on within the tomb.

From grotto grove and shrine
Saints from their icons fade,
Their presences withdrawn;
Meanings from words are dead
The springs gone under the hill.

Inviolate in dream
The mysteries still are shown,
The dead are living still;
But bring them back none may
Who wakes into this day.

1967

Hieros Gamos

I DID not think to see them once again,
For what could bring into an old woman's dream
Canova's immarcescible marble lovers?
But, glimpsed and gone,
I knew what each in other adores in that enamoured smiling
    gaze.
They need no mirror of art whose bodies invest immortal joy,
Love for ever beholding beauty in imagination's sight.

It is said that some born blind
Can with sensitive finger-tips perceive the light,
All senses grown one sense, as angels, full of eyes;
Their hands do not possess nor mouths consume
Whose knowledge is the beloved being, and whose being, bliss;
Cupid and Psyche in their trance. Oblivion veiled too soon
From my ignorant animal sleep that nuptial mystery.

A Dream of Roses

SO many roses in the garden
Of last night's dream, and all were golden—
Ophelia's flowers of love forsaken,
Yellow rose of luckless loving
Or the golden flower of wisdom?

There, in a night of late November
Fantasy had grown so many
In a garden I had planted
(So the dream told me) long before.
Yet I searched among the gold
For even one of true rose colour,
And found none; dream cannot lie,
None I found of love's true flower.

A BAD DREAM

TO enact the evil or the good, waking, we say,
  The will is free;
In dreams, all we conceive, reality.
No limit there
To what we may do, what must endure to be.

I have born dream-children, living and dead,
Have been in prison, guilty of murder of persons
    unknown,
Submitted to known and unknown lovers; fled,
Sometimes stood my ground; found myself unclad,
Abandoned, or too late; travelled on railway-journeys
    up and down
The long tracks of night; lost my companions, my
    luggage or my way,
Been carried out to sea,, seen galleons drown
With men aboard them, without a qualm.
Once in an aeroplane
That broke up in mid air, faced death, but floated down
Safe on some bright Mediterranean shore.

But an abortion
Of some misbegotten thing I would not own,
Parasite by no will of mine implanted in me
By some inadvertency,
How, when or by whom I did not know,
But for which I was, nevertheless, to blame,
—Yet last night it was so.
I who fear neither death nor sorrow fear the low,
To be dragged down
Where woman lies apathetic under lust,
In unregarded acts perpetuating woe;
And, waking, knew myself debased
In that world where the imagined is the real.

What's done by flesh and blood cannot be undone;
From acts of dream, waking, we are free.
But every life's a dream lived out
And every dream a looking-glass
Where what has been enacted, or may be,
Wears semblance of its reality.
My night's degrading fantasy
I, or some other who is myself
In that humanity all share,
Whose one dream interpenetrates
Under the full tide of sleep
All secret cells of misery or despair,
At some time suffered, to imprint
That record in the dreaming mind
Whose single fall we all enact
Whose undivided guilt we bear.

'I did not mean it', children cry,
'Not guilty', thief and murderer plead,
Invoking in that bewildered lie
Some true self innocent of their deed,
Some true self other than we are;
For there is hope that we may be
Forgiven, who know not what we do.
Oedipus, type of human guilt,
Who unawares his father slew,
As many in dream have done unblamed,
Without will's knowledge or consent,
Pleaded man's ignorance of what the gods knew.
Self-knowledge drove him from his throne
To suffer for the unwitting act,
To travel exile's endless way;
And yet, 'Know thyself', the Greeks say.

But in our time
The ivory gates of sleep are down,
And what Apollo hid from Oedipus,
Freud's censor cancelled from the Book of Life,

We, who would be as gods, must own:
Assume the guilt of unenacted crime
Committed beyond that broken door.
The Angel's voice cries, 'Sleep no more'.
And all for us must be despair
And vain our prayer to be forgiven,
Our trust in time's oblivion,
Our hope to reach the golden clime
Unless some sleeper someday wake
As at a trumpet's sound, from what we are
As to each day we wake absolved from dream.

Bank's Head, 12 May 1969

The Oval Portrait: Jessie Wilkie

(1880–1973)

AT eighteen, you stood for this faded photograph,
Your young hand awkwardly holding the long skirt
Over the light foot no trammeling at your heels could stay,
The constricting blouse framing in the eighteen-nineties
The young girl whose round sweet face,
Soft shining curls piled above fine brows and wild-bird's eyes
Has such a proud air of freedom and happy heart.

You were in love, that day,
Only with the beautiful world, that lay,
You thought, in your life's untold story,
As you, fledged for womanhood, ready to soar,
Stood poised before the camera's dark glass
Untouched by the shadow sorrow casts before
On all such inviolate light-heartedness.

Those young eyes, unfaded by your ninety years
Still saw in each day earth's wonders new-begun,
Each yesterday a leaf sinking into a dark pool
Of a swift sky-reflecting burn.
All for you was always the first time, or the last,
Every parting forevermore, but free each happy return
Of memory's unforgiveness, memory's remorse.

Your spirit fast in time's jesses, still you turned
On death's camera obscura that proud look,
Expectant, though not unafraid; after his first stroke
'I was interested', you said; as the goshawk,

Its hood lifted then drawn down again
Over the golden eyes, is restless to go free
On unencumbered wings home to its wilderness.

Her Room

AT first, not breathed on,
Not a leaf or a flower knew you were gone,
Then, one by one,

The little things put away,
The glass tray
Of medicines empty,

The poems still loved
Long after sight failed
With other closed books shelved,

And from your cabinet
Remembrances to one and another friend
Who will forget

How the little owl, the rose-bowl,
The Brig-o'Doone paperweight,
The Japanese tea-set

Lived on their shelf, just here,
So long, and there,
Binding memories together,

Binding your love,
Husband and daughter in an old photograph,
Your woven texture of life

A torn cobweb dusted down,
Swept from the silent room
That was home.

With a Wave of Her Old Hand

WITH a wave of her old hand
She put her past away,
Ninety years astray
In time's fading land,

With that dismissive gesture
Threw off pretence,
Rose to her proud stature,
Had done with world's ways,

Had done with words,
Closed her last written book
To ponder deeper themes
In unrecorded dreams.

The Leaf

'HOW beautifully it falls', you said,
As a leaf turned and twirled
On invisible wind upheld,
How airily to ground
Prolongs its flight.

You for a leaf-fall forgot
Old age, loneliness,
Body's weary frame,
Crippled hands, failing sense,
Unkind world and its pain.

What did that small leaf sign
To you, troth its gold
Plight 'twixt you and what unseen
Messenger to the heart
From a fair, simple land?

YOUR gift of life was idleness,
As you would set day's task aside
To marvel at an opening bud,
Quivering leaf, or spider's veil
On dewy grass in morning spread.
These were your wandering thoughts, that strayed
Across the ever-changing mind
Of airy sky and travelling cloud,
The harebell and the heather hill,
World without end, where you could lose
Memory, identity and name
And all that you beheld, became,
Insect wing and net of stars
Or silver-glistering wind-born seed
For ever drifting free from time.
What has unbounded life to do
With body's grave and body's womb,
Span of life and little room?

Acacia Tree

DAY by day the acacia tree
⠀⠀With gold of noon and evening sun
Through airy quivering leaves made play
In shadow underleaf, and gay
Mirrors tossing blades of light
Various before your failing sight.

Four pigeons plumed in rose and gray
Browsed spring buds of the tree's crown
And heavy white and fragrant flowers
To petal-fall in summer hung
Until mid-August's dulling leaves
Began to cast their yellow coin.

As time for you ran swift away
Moment by moment, day to night,
Nature's illuminated book,
No two moving hours the same,
Lay always open at one page
Where Tree in its long present stood,
September day by golden day.
Only before eyes new-born,
Eyes fading, does the mystery stay,
A presence neither come nor gone.

Binah

LIFELONG the way—
　　I never thought to reach her throne
In darkness hidden, starless night
Her never-lifted veil;
Too far from what I am
That source, sacred, secret from day;
But, suddenly weeping, remembered
Myself in her embrace,
In her embrace who was my own
Mother, my own mother, in whose womb
Human I became.
Not far, I found, but near and simple as life,
Loved in the beginning, beyond praise
Your mothering of me in flesh and blood.
Deep her night, but never strange
Who bore me out of the kind animal dark
Where safe I lay, heart to heartbeat, as myself
Your stream of life carrying me to the world.
Remote your being as the milky way,
Yet fragrance not of temple incense nor symbolic rose
Conforted me, but your own,
Whose soft breasts, nipples of earth, sustained me,
Mortal, in your everlasting arms.
Known to the unborn, to live is to forget
You, our all,
Whose unseen sorrowing face is a farewell,
Forgotten forgiver of forgetfulness.
Lifelong we seek that longed-for unremembered place.

Turner's Seas

WE call them beautiful,
   Turner's appalling seas, shipwreck and deluge
Where man's contraptions, mast and hull,
Lurch, capsize, shatter to driftwood in the whelming surge and
      swell,
Men and women like spindrift hurled in spray
And no survivors in those sliding glassy graves.
Doomed seafarers on unfathomed waters,
We yet call beautiful those gleaming gulphs that break in foam,
Beautiful the storm-foreboding skies, the lurid west,
Beautiful the white radiance that dissolves all.
What recognition from what deep source cries
Glory to the universal light that walks the ever-running waves,
What memory deeper than fear, what recollection of
      untrammelled joy
Our scattered falling drops retain of gleaming ocean's unending
      play?

I WENT out in the naked night
   And stood where you had often stood,
And called you where the winter moon
Over Canna harbour rode
Clear of the sheltering wind-bent trees
Above the quivering Pleiades
Where once at anchor rocked your boat.

The mountain isles changeless and still
As memory's insubstantial strand:
May not the living and the dead

Meet where dreaming spirit turns
To the sea-wracked remembered shore,
Revisiting this welcoming door,
Crushed shells beneath your grounding keel?

The moonlit waters of the bay
Move under the December stars
Between the shores of earth and dream.
In the unending Now of night,
In being's one unbroken theme
Your presence and my present meet:
I hold my transient breath to hear
The crunch of shells beneath your feet.

CROSSING the sound I summoned you in thought
To look out of my eyes at sea and sky,
Soft clouds sheltering those hills that once you knew
And sea-paths where you sailed,
The white birds following your boat from isle to isle.
Would it have seemed to you still beautiful, this world?
Or from that other state
Do you discern a darkness in our light,
The cloud of blood that veils our skies,
And in the labouring wings of hungry gulls
The weight of death? If it be so,
Dear love, I would not call you back
To bear again the heaviness of earth
Upon the impulse of your joy,
Locked in a living skull your thought,
Your vision shut with human eyes.

EIDER afloat in the bay,
 Cloud-capped isles far out,
This thyme-sweet turf I tread,
Real under my feet,

These were your world,
Your loved and known;
Can you recall to mind
Wrack-strewn shore and tide-wet stone?

I seek you in wave-wrought shell,
In wild bird's eye:
What country have the dead
But memory?

We who travel time
Call past and gone
Remembered days that those who dream
Call home.

ALL that is:
 The unbroken surface of the sea
Bears ships and isles,
Shelduck and eider in the bay;
Wings soar, wild voices cry.

Shining waves
Cast up fresh shells
On the sweet turf that covers the fine sand
Of innumerable gleaming lives.
Light fills all space
And all life joy,
All shores the sea; no place
For what has ceased to be.

BLUE butterflies' eyed wings,
Eyed buzzard high in blue sky,
Mountain isles blue veiled
In fleeting shade of fleeting cloud,
Of these I am the I.

PETAL of white rose
And rosy shell
Cast up by the tide:
Who can tell
This burnet sweetness
From memory,
From the deep sea
Record of a life
Shaped by the restless wave.

Kore

ONCE more
The yellow iris on the wrack-strewn shore
Blooms in our midsummer
Whose root is in that realm
Where the dead are
Everywhere underfoot
Where the salt of the sea makes sweet the grass of the land.
Among the roots of the turf the fine sea-sand
Of innumerable broken shells
Makes fertile root and flower.
Bright forms return:
Not once, but in multitude is shown
In signature of living gold the mystery
Of immortal joy.

Short Poems

POLLUTED tide,
Desecrated earth destroyed:
Yet one green leaf opens for the heart
The shelter of a great forest.

OVAL the golden moon
Hangs in the evening sky
Filling the bay with light,
So near,
If I could clear my sight,
Cast body away,
I would be here.

BANKED winter cloud,
Clear Northern sky
And the flash of Oighsgear light:
One far star
Poignant as joy
Signals for ever.

STILL skies, still seas
So like a memory lie
In mind's eye
It may be you return
Dreaming you sail these isles
To find these isles your dream

ALL things new
But I: no shadow
The gods cast,
But I my past.

AND that was all his life,
His share of days,
Says the grave;
You need not fear he lies
With another,
For him no more
Than the one life I spoiled for him;
And I live on.

IF I choose remorse
Of a heart inured to pain
It is because forgiveness would revive
Joy and love
To suffer all again.

ONCE I heard your voice
And now no word:
How are we immortal
On whom silence falls?

If you have ceased
Then I too already of the dead:
We are eternal
Or even now are not.

My feet in the ever-moving sea:
The same cold waves
Carried us to this shore.
Time joins us still, and space
And living water.

I breathe the air you have breathed,
See the sky you have seen,
Drink the water of the one life,
Am what you have been.

A rainbow, beautiful and clear light,
Whose span, at certain times, a way
Opens, I saw today,
On your far grave its radiant foot.

The Poet Answers the Accuser

NO matter what I am,
For if I tell of winter lightning, stars and hail,
Of white waves, pale Hebridean sun,
It is not I who see, who hear, who tell but all
Those cloud-born drops the scattering wind has blown
To be regathered in the stream of ocean,
The many in the one;
For these I am,
Water, wind and stone I am,
Gray birds that ride the storm and the cold waves I am,
And what can my words say,
Who am a drop in ocean's spray,
A bubble of white foam,
Who am a breath of wandering air,
But what the elements in me cry
That in my making take their joy,
In my unmaking go their way?
I am, but do not know, my song,
Nor to what scale my sense is tuned
Whose music trembles through me and flows on.
A note struck by the stars I am,
A memory-trace of sun and moon and moving waters,
A voice of the unnumbered dead, fleeting as they—
What matter who I am?

Winter Paradise

NOW I am old and free from time
How spacious life,
Unbeginning unending sky where the wind blows

The ever-moving clouds and clouds of starlings on the wing,
Chaffinch and apple-leaf across my garden lawn,
Winter paradise
With its own birds and daisies
And all the near and far that eye can see,
Each blade of grass signed with the mystery
Across whose face unchanging everchanging pass
Summer and winter, day and night.
Great countenance of the unknown known
You have looked upon me all my days,
More loved than lover's face,
More merciful than the heart, more wise
Than spoken word, unspoken theme
Simple as earth in whom we live and move.

Wind

COMPANIONLESS,
Without trace you are,
Without identity,
Without person or place,
Without name or destination,
Unbeginning, unending, unresting,
Are but speed and motion,
Crying without voice,
Without memory lamenting,
Without grief moaning, without anger storming,
Singing without joy, whistling to no-one:
Signifying nothing wind
You are yet of my kind,
Habitant of the same hills,
Wanderer over the same waters,
Beater against cliff-face,

We are the one world's way,
Move in the universal courses;
You blow over,
Breath through me always.

Cloud

NEVER alone
   While over unending sky
Clouds move for ever.
Calling them beautiful
Humanity is in love with creatures of mist.
Born on the wind they rest,
Tenuous, without surface,
Passive stream from shape to shape,
Being with being melting breast with cloudy breast.
Ah could we like these
In freedom move in peace on the commotion of the air,
Never to return to what we are.
Made, unmade, remade, at rest in change,
From visible to invisible they pass
Or gather over the desolate hills
Veils of forgetfulness,
Or with reflected splendour evening gray
Charged with fiery gold and burning rose,
Their watery shapes shrines of the sun's glory.

AFTERNOON sunlight plays
   Through trailing leaves I cannot see,
Stirred by a little wind that mixes light and leaf

To filter their quiet pattern on my floor.
Not real, Plato said, the shadowy dancers
Imponderable,
Somewhere beyond, the light; but I am old,
Content with these shadows of shadows that visit me,
Present unsummoned, gone without stir.

So angels, it may be.

B RIGHT cloud,
Bringer of rain to far fields,
To me, who will not drink that waterfall nor feel
Wet mist on my face,
White gold and rose
Vision of light,
Meaning and beauty immeasurable.
That meaning is not rain, nor that beauty mist.

H ARVEST of learning I have reaped,
Fruits of many a life-time stored,
The false discarded, proven kept,
Knowledge that is its own reward—
    No written page more true
    Than blade of grass and drop of dew.

Striven my partial self to bind
Within tradition great and whole,
Christendom's two thousand years,
Wisdom's universal mind—

No doctrine heart can heal
As cloudless sky and lonely hill.

Now I am old my books I close
And forget religion's ties,
Untrammelled the departing soul
Puts out of mind both false and true,
    Distant hills and spacious skies,
    Grass-blade and morning dew.

INTO what pattern, into what music have the spheres
   whirled us,
Of travelling light upon spindles of the stars wound us,
The great winds upon the hills and in hollows swirled us,
Into what currents the hollow waves and crested waters,
Molten veins of ancestral rock wrought us
In the caves, in the graves entangled the deep roots of us,
Into what vesture of memories earth layer upon layer
      enswathed us
Of the ever-changing faces and phases
Of the moon to be born, reborn, upborn, of sun-spun days
Our arrivals assigned us, our times and our places,
Sanctuaries for all love's meetings and partings, departings
Healings and woundings and weepings and transfigurations?

BEHIND the lids of sleep
   In what clear river
Do the maimed, the misshapen
Bathe slender feet?
From what sky, what mountain
Do these waters pour
That wash away the stain
Of the world's mire?

On what journey
Does the night-traveller go

In quest of what lost treasure?
In what holy land
The mysteries shown,
Meaning beyond words and measure,
In what cave what ear of wheat?

Behind closed lids
The toil-worn stray
In fields not sown.
In childless arms a child is laid,
And, stilled with awe,
A bodiless mourner hears
A harmony too deep for senses dulled with pain.

By secret ways
The old revisit some long-vanished house
Once home, open a door
Where the long dead, made young again,
Offer the food of dream
That none may taste that would return.

Each to our own place
We go where none may follow
Nor hurt nor harm
The gentle wanderer whose waking days
Are exile, and whose slumbering form,
Vesture of soul clay cannot soil
Nor years deface,
Shabby and travel-worn.

Columbines

FINDING in a friend's garden columbines
It was as if they were those my mother grew,
And above all those coloured like a shell
Of rosy pearl seemed hers,

Returned, in all their freshness, from her garden
To remind me of, it should have been, happy days
When I was sheltered by her love and shared her flowers.
But by the vague bitter sorrow that arose
Out of the shadowy present of the past
I knew that it had not been so.
Wilful and unloving had been the daughter
My mother made, and all her flowers in vain
Offering her life to mine.
What did I hope to find when I turned away from her
Towards a cold future, now my sum of years,
From the unprized only love earth had for me,
Demeter's for her lost Persephone.

High Summer

GLADLY I would be again
Where I began,
Undone the years between.

Flowers in this summer bloom
Now as before all to come,
All that has been.

O my wandering soul
Are you still
One who before my days was beautiful?

What signifies the dream
Of time's life-long travail
Now it is gone?

Do I return
To the presence of the garden
The same, or not the same?

The Fateless Ones

TO the fateless ones
All is given,
They ask no other
Day, no other sun
To rise on daisies
More white than these,
They leave no trace
Of past or future,
Being their own place,
Have no elsewhere;
Their sparrows are angels
Of the one
In all things boundless.

Monessie Gorge

1

SEEN from the train
Brown, brown water, swift
Bubbles of foam, and as I pass I am
That stream, am one
With the continuous, swept on
My course, the pouring river
In its shelving gorge for ever
Wearing its rocks away.

2

LIVE on in me, remembered ones,
I am your future and your memory
Who, within this ever-moving now
At rest in change, wore, as I wear,
The seamless dress of earth and sea and sky.
One in the long unbroken flow
We who have been are one another for ever
Whose voices to the stars must cry and cry
In sorrow and in ecstasy, 'I am'.

3

'I AM the stream', I said:
And yet not I the seer,
The running water,
The joy unbounded.

4

IT crossed my mind
That death might be like this
Opening, this boundless
Coming forth, to say
'This river is I', to extend
Suddenly like air,
To be everywhere
Like sky beyond vault of cloud,
Not less myself, but more than I.
Yet I had lost my situation in time and place
And wondered, after,
Who it was who had
Been I when I said
In fleeting joy 'I am the river'.

My Mother's Birthday

7 November 1880

1

NOVEMBER rain with thin fingers tapping
In the wind-gusts against my window-pane,
You have not changed since, near a century ago,
Curled in her cot, my mother heard you about the house,
New-born to the familiar strangeness of wind and rain,
Earth's chill northern winters hers; only a mile or two away.
But I whom tonight you summon am not she
Who in my turn have heard your wordless elemental voices.
You are what you always were, but we
Do not return, though a myriad follow us;
Our drop of life a destiny, our tears
Fall not from the ever-forming and re-forming mist
That blows about the hills, but from the clouds
Of another mystery: we love, we die.

2

I USED to watch you, sleeping,
Your once brown shining ringlets gray.
It was your way to lie
Your knees high, your old twisted hands
In the archaic posture of the unborn,
Raised to your pillow, and I could see
How in the cradle you had lain
For comfort of your own warmth curled up
Like those poor children covered by the robin
With leaves, or under blanket of snow the snowdrop.
Your neglected childhood told its story
In the way you composed yourself for the grave.
Why had not your mother, bending over her baby,
Ninety years ago, wrapped you warm?
I, your daughter, felt pity

For that unwanted babe, for comfort too long
    ago, too far away.

Returning from Church

THAT country spire—Samuel Palmer knew
    What world they entered, who,
Kneeling in English village pew,
Were near those angels whose golden effigies
        looked down
From Gothic vault or hammer-beam.
Grave sweet ancestral faces
Beheld, Sunday by Sunday, a holy place
Few find who, pausing now
In empty churches, cannot guess
At those deep simple states of grace.

Campanula

THIS morning, waking
    But not yet remembering it was I
Who saw in my window white campanula stars
Against white mistiness
Curving like a shining hill against the panes,
Remembered or discerned
A way of being those immaculate flowers
Were part of, once, some house

[131]

Of elegance and kindness, where I had been,
It seemed, or still remained, until the day
Opened the present and closed
That other time and place the flowers lingered in
A little longer than I. Another decade
It had been, or another life, whose ways
Were fine and clear as these
White visitants from a house of presences forgotten.

Winds

I HAVE heard all day the voices
On the hills the loud winds
Utter from no place, clamour
Of bodies of air, speeding, whirling
Stream of invisible
Elements crying that are not,
Were, may be, living
The fields of the grass, lifting
Leaves of the forests, are not, have been, would be
Breath of all sentient beings, long lamentation
For living and loving and knowing, states of being
The wandering winds cannot
Discover for ever for all their seeking and wailing.

Medea

ANGUISH and revenge made visible, her serpents lifted
Medea above pity and horror of the enacted
Crime; murderess to herself most cruel,
Absolute in power of absolute loss,
Invulnerable by human justice or human hate,
Apollo whose ancestral fire seethed in her veins
Snatched among the gods who acknowledge only
The truth of life, fulfilled in her
To the last bitter blood-drop of her being.
On amphora and crater apotheosis
Has raised into the myths of Greece the barbarous
Wronged woman whose outstretched parting hand
Warns that there are furies among the immortals,
That anguish is an avenging frenzy
Of passionate love that slaughters her own children.
What could earth-bound Jason who rated calculation
above the gods
Answer Medea departing on the dragon-chariot of her
desolation?

Canna's Basalt Crags

TO their grey heights they rise,
The basalt crags thus far into blue air
Stayed where force into form no farther lifted
Archaic columns of fire frozen to stone
Temple where winds will sing, clouds gather
Till sun and ice of summers and winters totter
Their rocky hexagons. In vein and crevice
Wild bees find sweetness of wild thyme

Whose fine roots unfasten crystal by crystal, grain by grain
Boulders that tumble
Down slope whose stunted hazel leans to the prevailing
    weather.
Geometric unseen shapers limn
Wind-rounded waterworn contours of the isles
To the least lens winter-green moss turns to the sun
And bend of sedge a-quiver in current of air that lifts
Seabirds as rock-face turns gale from its course.
                              What part in this
Concord of wisdom's unerring agents by whose design
Fall of farthest star by ever so little mountain and grass-blade
    stirs,
Sand-grain and rain-drop poised to fall
To the wet hill's trickling water-track, has a thought
That stays no tempest, leaves no trace
Of seer on seen, and yet knows all?

Short Poems

WHAT does this day bestow?
Beauty of sparse snow
Whose wet flakes touch
The soil, then vanish

FROST-RIME edges blades of grass,
The garden blackbird crosses
The motionless air
To the rigid hawthorn.

MOON golden towards the full,
Summits of pine afloat
Over level mist, the hills
Cloudlike, adrift.

LONDON air dims
Blue of a cold spring sky,
Bricks as usual, and the morning news;
But rook and robin tell other things.

THESE watery diamond spheres
Fall, quench in soil
Thirst of all dead who toil
In Hades' house, where roots
Drink from the skies.

ON its way I see
The anew-created
Garden as old as woman; to me
These daisies in the grass are shown, these
Birds in the apple-tree:
Is my sin, then,
Forgiven?

FOREST is multitude,
But one tree all, one apple-bud
Opens the flower of the world, infinite
Golden stamens and rose petals, here.

AH, many, many are the dead
Who hold this pen and with my fingers write:
What am I but their memory
Whose afterlife I live, who haunt
My waking and my sleep with the untold?

MY sight with the clouds'
Unimpeded rest in changing moves
Across the sky: the aged in endless
Unbecoming are at peace.

I COULD have told much by the way
But having reached this quiet place can say
Only that old joy and pain mean less
Than these green garden buds
The wind stirs gently.

Six calices yellow gold,
Fire-gold one, seven
Lamps of the Almighty, flame
Today in my garden, blown
Poppies in the wind.
In the beginning kindled they
Burn on.

Flower, memory—
My old eyes behold
Late narcissus' green-gold pheasants' eye,
Petals fresh pleated; scent
Immemorial. Now
Is all my springs'
Sorrow, joy.

Under these hills too high and bare
For love or war
I live in a green place without a story:
Sun, cloud, wind; beyond
My gate the simple fields that Adam tilled.

From vague regions of sleep I come again
To a cottage in a green field, flowers
Many-coloured, wind, sky, stability of day.
Do the dead, in dreams astray
Seek in vain the gate that opens
Into this world each morning?

WHAT have I to regret
Who, being old,
Have forgotten who I am?
I have known much in my time
But now behold
Procession of slow clouds across my sky.

THIS little house
No smaller than the world
Nor I lonely
Dwelling in all that is.

YOUNG or old
What was I but a story told
By an unageing one?

TODAY as I
Looked up at the sky's great face
I saw the bright heavens gaze
Down upon me.

LIFELONG ago such days
Of travelling cloud and ceaseless wind
Sealed my flesh and blood
Native of wild hills.
Elsewhere sun and summer; here
High elementals of the air.

TODAY:
This leafy apple-tree, gray
And gentle sky where the winds stray
Among mothering clouds, soft
Breast where every thirst
Cools its burning, rests in changing
Mist and air, light.

I'VE read all the books but one
Only remains sacred: this
Volume of wonders, open
Always before my eyes.

IF, into this evening as the grass receives the dew
I could step out of myself on weightless feet
I would be with the grass-blades, the dew-gathers,
But cannot cross
The frontiers of their green kingdom cool and still
In my dense body
Walking this twilit grass towards the grave.

LAST night I seemed in your embrace,
And sorrowing because you were about to die
Pleaded with you from my soul
Soul's immortality. Today
I wake into my place,
You beyond death, I mortal.

DEAR ones in the house of the dead,
Can you forgive
An old woman who was your proud
Daughter, who now too late
Returns your love?

WHEN I woke up to the snow
Joy for a moment stirred in me:
Happy expectation of a Christmas-tree
Long ago.

WORLD:
Image on water, waves
Break and it is gone, yet
It was.

Descent Into Hades

INSTANTLY they are about me, presences
In multitude, invisible they surround, press
Close at heart: 'Tell, tell', they say, 'tell
'The untold of buried hearts that cannot rest
'Till emptied of all that through the dark blood flowed
'And pale tears shed.
'Our sorrow lives in you, sorrow and love
'Untellable, untold. Tell, tell', they say,
'Tell our secret who, unsatisfied,
'Inhabit now your heart, you who must speak
'The love we bore, the love we bear in you,
'In you, who must remember us, remember for us
'Who did not know our hearts, when there were days,
'Days when we might have given you our love
'Who would not know our hidden truth, now yours,
'Our life your life,
'Sorrow uncomforted and love unspoken;
'And you must love us now
'With our rejected loves that love on now in you,
'Bound in the bonds of pain,
'Of pain we caused,
'Cause of the only pain the dead can know,
'Who suffer us, who are at your mercy
'As you at ours.'

Now they are silent: they attend within
The writing of this page of life for them in blood
That gives them speech: my blood, my speech
I pour into their open pit, my chthonic heart.

Their flesh put off, I know them life to life,
Who am their life, they mine to the end of time,
My time which they bequeathed me to inhabit,
Whose lengthening years full circle turn
Back to the heart where they await.
I would beg my dead for mercy,
To bless with all their powerless wisdom, speechless grace,
Be blessed by them, and find beatitude
For them, and for myself, and for my children,
Who are their children, are their ancestors;
But not yet is heart's fill of sorrow shed
Whose tortuous veins bind us, dead and living, pain to pain.

Oracles

FROM their grave lion-mouths, oracles
  With angel-tongues outpour
Continuous the silent flood of time.
But we who cannot stem, but are that flow
Known only that we fall and fall
From source to abyss for ever.
Their serene wisdom is the book of life we write
In blood and ignorance, who are
Incomprehensible utterance of masks of dream.

The Chartres Annunciation

NO, that carved angel whose still smile
The sun reveals or shadow veils
Day and night through centuries
Is not her lover, towards whom she bends
Attentive, as he towards her inclines.
To her solitude he brings
His silent telling of world to world.
Flesh that from flesh conceives ignores
The mystery of god from god;
That angle-smile in sun-warmed stone
Intelligence of dream imparts,
Her mystery in whose human house
All children are the divine child.

My Father's Birthday

15 March 1880

HE remained silent on many things,
In his last years, he could not speak of
To wife or daughter who had never shared
Memories and hopes nearest his heart. Only with
    children he could
Share the simplicity of receiving from God
With gladness what each day brought,
The morning sun, the task he never refused.
His month was windy March, when coltsfoot flowers
Open their bright disks to receive the sun, or close
Against the chill and cloud of a harsh season.
On my childhood my father shone like an early sun,
Who in his old age closed his rays against the cold
Climate of a loveless house.

For the Visitors' Book

Canna House, 1975

For John and Margaret Campbell

THE cards that brighten the New Year,
A Christmas-tree grown in the wood,
The crimson curtains drawn, the owl
Whose porcelain holds a lamp to read
The music on the Steinway grand
Piano with its slipping scores
Of Couperin, Chopin and Ravel—
John and Margaret Campbell made
This room to house the things they treasure,
Records of Scotland's speech and song,
Lore of butterfly and bird,
And velvet cats step soft among
Learned journals on the floor.

More formal state across the hall,
The silver of the house displayed,
And ivory ladies, Chinese birds
Surveyed by Romney's General
Sir Archibald, whose following eyes
Seem with cool justice to appraise
Guests of the house who come and go.
His scarlet, silver order, sword,
Give him the advantage as he stands
Relaxed, Imperial Madras
His pictured background, ours a world
That now breeds few he would approve,
That kindly but commanding man
Who played the part his rank assigned
And governed by a law deemed just,
As Indian Arjuna before,
Taught by his god to act, though slain
And slayer were of equal worth.

The rule of duty had not changed
With other empire, other race,
Though oftener in our day ignored
By innovators, who to make
A new world would destroy old ways.

In Scotland it is Hogmanay
Most warms the feelings of the heart,
Religion older than the old,
The cycle of perpetual things
In years that pass and years to come.
Here children sing from memory
Ancestral island tunes that praise
Those best of loves that never change
Though new men bear their fathers' names,
Boatmen and herdsmen of these shores.
We feast on venison from a neighbouring hill
Under that Campbell general's eye,
The drone of pipes across the bay,
The pibroch 'Cattle of Kintail'
Played by the piper of the isle.

After Fifty-five Years

In memory of Germain d'Hangest

STILL in the now of then they remain,
But we who were with them cannot return
To where the dead await us in past times and places;
Yet the forgotten haunts us always,
Wears like a mask the façade of a house, murmurs to us
From trees whos branches sheltered us once,
Seeking to enter again the transience we inhabit.
Here in Montparnasse

Round the next corner I expect to meet
One who long ago
Opened for me invisible doors into the timeless
Fields of Elysium, or some more shadowy
Sanctuary of those who were. I did not guess,
Then, that I was myself that place,
Refuge too frail for all those moods and modes,
Insights, fleeting imagined joys
Of the spirit of life that always eludes, though near
As Balzac's imagined duchess to his door,
Or the child Marcel's coloured image of old France
Cast on the wall of an empty room, that yet
Was, or almost was, once here and now,
Sole refuge of memories.

Paris, August 1978

Whales

Written for a coffee-table book in aid of Greenpeace

UNDER the ever-moving, mighty dreams,
    You sound our seas,
Powers, strong angels of the world, thoughts
Of the undying one life, you rise
From what deep springs of ocean? Not yours
As our thoughts, who, slaughterous,
Have moved mountains to loose the Titans' fires
Wise gods of life locked underground.
We, of innocent immemorial green earth
Enact the suicide,
Maddened by fear of terrors we ourselves commit,
Ourselves we realize our own darkest prophecies:
'And the creatures which were in the sea, and had
        life, died'.

WHO listens, when in the concert-hall,
The great whispering-gallery
Vaulted ear of the encaverned god
Scattered in our multitude
Ebb and flow the waves of the world?
In deep ocean weed
Sways, like a caress,
Life's delicate responsive silia.
Sound passes like air
Over a field of grass, whose thousand ears
Bend to the wind, to the oracular voice
Ten thousand auricles attend
As the one hearer hears in all.

Published in the New Yorker in the 1940s.
Set to music by Marshall Bialosky, 1981

On a Shell-strewn Beach

WHAT are you looking for,
Hoping to find there
On the sea shore?
A marvellous shell
More bright than rainbow
Small as a pearl
And carved like the tower
Of a white cathedral.

[147]

What are you waiting for,
Tide after tide
On the shore of the ocean?
        I have come seeking
        The infinite cipher
        And sum of all wisdom
        Inscribed on a grain
        Of sand that can lie
        In the palm of my hand.

Have you searched in vain,
Waited in vain
On the white beaches?
        By every tide
        The white strand
        Is strewn with treasure,
        Shells without number
        Brighter than rainbow
        Formed in pools
        Deeper than dreams
        In purple water
        That teems with creation,
        I have found
        A myriad particles
        And each is all
        That can ever be told,
        But all are inscribed
        With a signature
        That I cannot read,
        Nor may I inhabit
        Towers of ivory
        And golden houses.

The Listener,
September 13th 1951

The Holy Isles

For William Irwin Thompson and all the friends he has
united in the abiding vision of Lindisfarne

LINDISFARNE

THOSE whose faces are turned always to the sun's rising
See the living light on its path approaching
As, over the glittering sea where in tide's rising and falling
The sea-beasts bask, on the Isles of Farne
Aidan and Cuthbert saw God's feet walking
Each day towards all who on world's shores await his coming.
There we too, hand in hand, have received the unending morning.

IONA

WHERE, west of the sun, our loved remembered home?
Columba's Eire from Iona's strand
Land-under-wave beyond last dwindling speck
That drops from sight the parting ship
As mourners watch wave after wave break.
Sight follows on its golden wake
A dream returning to its timeless source, the heart
Where all remains that we have loved and known.

Star of Bethlehem

HOW far
Must that star descend
From beyond the beyond beyond
Conceivable source
To darkest end?

[149]

The eternal child
Finds the here
And now always
Of the times and places
Where we are.

M Y day's plan to write
From gospel text on heaven,
But saw a wren flit
And then another, among jasmin
By the window, and forgot
Holy pages while in leaves unwritten
Messengers from the Kingdom.

As therefore the tares are gathered and burned in the fire;
so shall it be at the end of the world. Matt. 13.40

I T is in us they burn,
Those undying flames—
Over our night cities
Glare the dull red skies
Of the eternal Dis.

Implacable neon signs
Signal to the night
Trivial inanities,
But their true import
We know is otherwise.

City to city flare
Their beacons to the stars—
Mankind has loosed the power
Of the stolen fire
Whose seed is in the heart.

Destruction is within us
Who secretly delight
In violence, rape and murder,
Who while we prate of peace
Hurt and harm and hate.

'God cannot be so cruel'
We say, 'as to condemn us
To Hell!' who have ourselves
Built it and live in it:
'So shall it be' He said.

THE poet is of those
Who see but cannot be
In that holy place.

Vision of mirage trembles
In a dry wilderness
Of an elsewhere island.

Of garden and tree I have told,
Mountain and clear stream,
Remember, who may not enter

That ever-present kingdom
Where some I know and have known
Have been and are always,

Whose brightness from far away
Shines on my desert journey:
Yet I bear witness.

WHAT message from imagined Paradise
Can bring hope to us, whose daily news
Is of polluted forests, poisoned seas,
Of the polluted air, the clouds
Laden with sour vapours from our furnaces,
What can we hope or pray for that can heal these
Mortal wounds of our brief beloved earth?
There is no turning, no returning
For us, whose birth
Sets time on the move, first cause
Of all this consequence.
Implicit in each beginning is its end:
What poet can write
Of beauty truth and goodness in these days
(Or say rather, of what else?).
Oh, I know it all as well as any,
And yet I feel delight
As I look up into today's blue skies
Where the sun still gives light
And warmth (wisdom and love, Blake says)
And on this doomed decaying city rise
On the last days as on the first
These marvels inexhaustible and boundless.

Dream

I AM become a stranger to my dreams,
Their places unknown. A bridge there was
Over the lovely waters of the Tyne, my mother
Was with me, we were almost there,
It seemed, but in that almost opened up a valley
Extending and expanding, wind-sculptured sand;
Dry its paths, a beautiful waterless waste
Without one green leaf, sand-coloured behind closed eyes.
That film shifts, but the arid place remains
When day returns. Yet we were still going towards the Tyne,
That green river-side where childhood's flowers
Were growing still, my mother and I, she dead,
With me for ever in that dream.

To the Sun

1

SUN, great giver of all that is,
Once more I return from dream to your times and places
As geese wing over London in this morning's dawn
Before the human city invades your immaculate spaces.
Sun, greatest of givers, your speeding rays
Weave again familiar quotidian things, epiphanies
Of trees, leaves, wings, jewelled rain, shining wonders.
Your golden mask covers the unknown
Presence of the awakener of all eyes
On whose blinding darkness none can gaze.
Clouds and hills and gardens and forests and seas,
High-rise buildings, dust and ordure, derelict and broken things

Receive alike from holiest, purest source
Meaning and being, messages each morning brings
To this threshold where I am.
Old, I marvel that I have been, have seen
Your everything and nothing realm, all-giving sun.

2

How address you, greatest of givers,
God, angel, these words served once, but no longer
Apollo's chariot or Surya's horses imaged in stone
Of Konarak, glorious metaphor of the advancing power
Of the unwearied sun from the eternal East. My time
Has other symbols, speeding light waves, light-years, rays
Cycling for ever the boundless sphere of space,
Vast emptiness of what is or is not,
Unsolid matter's equivocal seeming—
Science only another grandiose myth we have dreamed,
Ptolemaic or Copernican, or Einstein's paradigm
Less real than those magnificent stone horses
As light triumphs over darkness for yet one more day.
But no myth, as before our eyes you are, or seem!
In your numinous glory I have seen you rise
From beyond the Farne Isles casting your brilliance
Over cold northern seas, or over the seas of Greece,
Have seen your great rim rising from India's ocean.
As you circle the earth birds sing your approach each morning,
New flowers open in wilderness, gardens, waste-places,
All life your retinue, as before all eyes you summon,
Greatest of givers, your heavens outspread
Our earth's vast and minute spaces, to each the whole,
And today I receive yet again from your inexhaustible treasury
Of light, this room, this green garden, my boundless universe.

3

ANCESTRAL sun, do you remember us,
Children of light, who behold you with living eyes?
Are we as you, are you as we? It seems
As if you look down on us with living face:
Who am I who see your light but the light I see,
Held for a moment in the form I wear, your beams.

I have stood on shores of many seas,
Of lakes and rivers, and always over the waters,
Across those drowning gulphs of fear
Your golden path has come to me
Who am but one among all who depart and return.

Blinding sun, with your corona of flames, your chasms of fire,
Presence, terrible theophany,
Am I in you, are you in me,
Infinite centre of your unbounded realm
Whose multitudes sing Holy, Holy, Holy?
Do you go into the dark, or I?

4

NOT that light is holy, but that the holy is the light—
Only by seeing, by being, we know,
Rapt, breath stilled, bliss of the heart.
No microscope nor telescope can discover
The immeasurable: not in the seen but in the seer
Epiphany of the commonplace.
A hyacinth in a glass it was, on my working-table,
Before my eyes opened beyond beauty light's pure living flow.
'It is I', I knew, 'I am that flower, that light is I,
'Both seer and sight'.
Long ago, but for ever; for none can un-know
Native Paradise in every blade of grass,
Pebble, and particle of dust, immaculate.
'It has been so and will be always', I knew,

No foulness, violence, ignorance of ours
Can defile that sacred source:
Why should I, one of light's innumerable multitude,
Fear in my unbecoming to be what for ever is?

Testimony

1

SO late, for whom, to whom
Do I speak, for the old, for the young,
Of for no-one? To none
Or these—from the everlasting to the unborn, undying
I speak, who am alone
In a time and place where none
Will find me, who am already gone,
When you, whoever you may be,
Old, young, in the middle of life's way
Are with me in this no-place, no-time
Unbounded, where each is, who for a moment holds,
As I now, in your heart, the world.
As you I am
Heart's cup, filled for a moment
From ocean and air and light,
This body, this cup that overflows
With the one Presence, will be gone,
Dissolved again, as again and again
Drop in the ocean,
Will have become you, no more
This woman whose hand writes words not mine,
Bequeathed by multitude of the once living
Who knew, loved, understood and told
Meanings passed down
To the yet to come, whose faces I shall not see,
Yet whom, as I write these words, I already am.

2

WHAT can I tell you, future ones,
Who am old, who was young,
Was a child, who was
In my boundless here and now as you?
My writing hand bears witness from my dark world
In your dark time to come
To heart's delight.
You who will be, and I,
The one heart's-blood shed
Over and over, blood of begetting
Seeking always the bliss of being
Ever-presence of the ever-living,
What can I tell but the one mystery
That here and now for me
Is this bright sun, this morning sky.

3

I AM old, I am alone,
As others are alone this night,
In the small circle of my light,
Within the four walls of my winter room,
Within my skin, withered with time,
Within my heart, beating its way
Through yet another day towards time's end,
Least lonely when alone,
Soon not to be; yet the all-embracing,
In silence eloquent, present in absence, ageless,
Young in the old, old in the new-born
Everywhere and nowhere, is fleet, is gone,
Now as I write, is heart-to heart, is mine.